DICK LEE'S

KEEP

THE ART OF TRAINING

FIGHTING COCKS

R. H. Lee,

The Veteran Cocker and Trainer.

Preface.

To the Reader:—In compiling this little manual entitled, "Dick Lee's Keep," we have added a lot of rules of the cock pit, also the diseases of game fowl and an assorted lot of remedies that have been tested and proven to be beneficial. We have also added a condition for dogs from one of the most accomplished trainers in America, with the worst diseases of dogs and remedies for same. In addition to these very important features will be found the new revised Police Gazette Rule for fighting dogs in America.

We will say in conclusion that Dick Lee's treatise on game cocks was compiled with great care, and is the result of half a century's experience. Mr. Lee is now in his seventy-first year and has never been accused of a dishonorable act, and well deserves the confidence of his friends and backers.

It is with the desire that this little book of valuable information will be of interest to the fraternity, is respectfully submitted by the

•   PUBLISHER.

The Art of
Training
Fighting Cocks.

The art of training fighting-cocks has received the attention of the world's greatest scientists, men who care nothing for sport, but who are in search of knowledge which may in some manner benefit mankind. They have been amazed at the amount of severe punishment a well-conditioned gamecock can undergo and yet retain his strength.

I have a mental photograph of battles between these wonderful fighters —broken legs, eyes knocked out, backs uncoupled, necks wryed, wings broken

1

and lungs filled with blood and spouting at every pore, and they fight on with courage that challenges the admiration of the world.

The sport has been legislated against in every State; it has been driven from the palaces of kings to the subcellar of the dive, yet no matter where these noble warriors may meet to do battle, they will, so long as man admires that courage with which the Creator deemed wise not to endow the masters of the world, occupy a warm spot in the hearts of men.

The conditioning of fighting-cocks means simply to harden the flesh. The only way in which this can be accomplished is by physicing, feeding and exercising. And the simplest way is always the best. Volumes could be written upon the subject, but they usually confuse the reader, and he throws them away in disgust.

The age demands concentration and condensation. Oftentimes a few lines will state a fact or chronicle an event of importance, and the eager will

know how and where to follow up
the suggestion.

Some trainers profess to have two
methods by which they are guided,
i. e., one way for short and another
for long gaffs. I have fought cocks
with every known style of weapons,
and am convinced that if a cock is in
condition he can fight as well with
slashers as with short gaffs. The
feeder should bear in mind that all
game cocks are not fighters. And no
matter how well trained they may be
they will not be able to whip a real
fighter. You can not make racers
out of cart horses, and you can not
make fighters out of sluggish, inact-
ive game-cocks.

THE TRAINING QUARTERS.

The training quarters should be
dry, well ventilated, with plenty of
light, and arranged in such a manner
as to be made comfortable both in
winter and summer. Nothing so
quickly dulls cocks as to be poorly
housed. If the weather is excessively
cold I would advise the trainer to

darken the room, as cocks will then sit down, thus keeping the legs warm, which is an important factor in conditioning fighting cocks.

The coops should be large and smooth inside, with a few holes bored in the tops to allow a free passage of air. The fronts should be made of laths, placed about one inch apart. A great many feeders leave openings in the front on which to hang feeding cups. This is, in my opinion, wrong, as cocks become used to each other, which causes them to lose the vim and dash with which they are naturally endowed; besides, game-cocks are usually nervous, and will frequently lose their appetites through fretting.

The old saying that a game-cock "would rather fight than eat" is a true one in this case. Of course they will eat when starved, but the continual fretting will impair the digestion, which is as injurious as to be weakened by hunger.

The feeding cups should be made of soft pine, about 3 inches in depth and 4 inches square, tapering down to a point, thus enabling the cock to eat his allotment of food, which should be placed inside the coop, fastened in such a manner as not to be turned over. Cocks often waste food but if it is inside the coop it will give them some exercise in scratching for the grains.

I have frequently cooped cocks that would not eat from a cup, but when the food was thrown into the coop they would work like Trojans to get it, and they nearly always worked themselves into condition.

The feeding cups should not be used, as they make the cock's beaks sore, which is a disadvantage in fighting.

SELECTING THE FIGHTERS.

Great care should be taken in selecting cocks to fight. When you examine the fowl on walks they usually look well, but the majority of farmers who are entrusted with the care of fighting cocks value a four cent stalk of "Flat Head Dutch Cabbage" more than your game cock.

and an occasional smash across the back with the hard end of a garden rake does not ruffle the feathers a great deal and in a few days the cock may look all right, but he is weak, and even in sparring he does not turn black in the face (which is an indication of weakness or an impaired constitution) and frequently winds up in his work as well as any in the coop; but after half an hour's cutting in the fight he suddenly becomes weak and you can not account for it.

A conditioned cock should be able to strike the last blow hard enough to kill his opponent. This he can not do if he has sustained an injury.

His trouble began the first time the granger caught him leading a family of egg producers into the cabbage patch. So it is better to walk only a few cocks and put them with people whom you have reason to believe will treat them well, than to walk a hundred and put them out with any one. I once walked sixteen cocks on a farm. I could have picked them all up in an hour. They were on the runs, but the country boys would congregate every Sunday and have a battle-royal with naked heels. The result was that I picked up only five out of the lot, and they were the worst duffers I ever handled. They were all game cocks but they could not fight. They looked well enough on the walk, but could neither fight nor get out of the way. I discovered after I had picked the cocks up that a howling evangelist had paid the locality a visit, and his rantings against such cruel (?) sport, was the reason that all my fighting cocks were not killed to make a "Roman Holiday." That was only one instance. I have lost a great many cocks on bad runs.

CLEANING THEM OUT.

The cocks which are to be shor n in the main should be kept up from twelve to fifteen days.

In cold weather cocks can be fougl t from 2 to 4 ounces heavier than in warm weather, and contrary to the opinions held by some cockers, it re-

quires more time in which to reduce
the weight of the cocks in winter
than it does in summer, consequently
it requires a few days more work with
them.

Fowls usually carry more flesh during the winter months than in summer.

The cocks should be rid of mites
and weighed as soon as brought in,
and the weight set down in a book,
and weighed every morning during
the course of training.

The coops should also be numbered
and the numbers on the coops should
correspond with those in the book.

The feeder can then see the decrease or increase in the weight.
They frequently lose from 4 to 6
ounces the first few days, and then
an ounce a day until they become
solid, and then they begin to rise in
weight, showing a healthy constitution. Sick cocks do not gain in
weight at any time.

A great deal depends upon the
proper cleaning out of the fowl. It
is really the most important part of a
trainer's work, and great care and

judgment is required at all seasons of the year.

I have used calomel for physicing, prepared in the following manner for fifty years, i. e., 25 grains of cream of tartar, 15 grains of Jalap made into pills, being moistened with sweet spirits of nitre and a little fresh butter. Mix until it becomes about as stiff as putty, then roll each pill in flour, and examine the cocks, marking each coop, whether its tenant is fat, lean or middling.

Having provided yourself with calomel tablets in the following sizes: 1 grain, 2 grain and 3 grain. For the fat cocks give the largest calomel tablet. Making an opening in the mixture of jalap, cream of tartar, nitre and butter with the point of a pen knife large enough to admit the tablet, take the cock in the following manner: placing your left foot upon a chair lay him on his breast across your leg, with his legs hanging behind, pressing gently yet firmly, with your left arm across his back, at the same time opening his beak with

your left front finger, pressing your
thumb back of his comb. The position is the most comfortable in which
you can place him and will enable
you to get the pill down his throat.
The "middling" cocks should have
the medium tablet, and of course the
lean fellows must be given the smal-
ler one.

Immediately after the pill has been
given, give each cock a tablespoonful
of sweetened water, made in the following manner: Take several slices
of toast(stale bread)and put them into an earthern vessel and pour a quart
of warm water over them, then add a
tablespoonful of sugar. Have the
floors of the coops cleaned and in an
hour or so you will see the effect of
the purgative. Wipe the coops out
and put in clean, dry straw from
which all the grain has been beaten.
The straw must be fresh, with no
musty smell. At night give each
cock a tablespoonful of cornmeal
m ish over which a spoonful of fresh
sw et milk has been poured. The
next morning wash the cock's feet

and legs with soap and warm water
and wipe them dry, then give each
cock a feed of corn bread moistened
with a teaspoonful of beef tea, made
from Liebig's Extract.

THE FOOD.

The corn bread is made as follows
(say for a fifteen cock main): Five
pounds of good corn meal, one dozen
fresh eggs, beaten well, yoke and
white together. Mix the meal and
eggs together, then use enough sweet
milk(boiled) to soften, and bake in
pie plates, making each cake about
one inch thick. Allow it to bake
slowly, and while warm cut it into
pieces about the size of a grain of
corn, and then spread out on a table
to dry. It will keep for a month or
more and be better than when fresh.

The oat bread is made in the same
manner and cut and dried the same.

The beef tea is made by putting a
half teaspoonful of the extract in a
pint of boiling water and allowing it
to cool. It should be used very sparingly throughout the course of train-

ing, except to thin cocks, as it is very fattening, though while cocks are going through the process of the purgative it is about the best and most strengthening article of diet that could be used during this critical period. I say critical because I have found that the only way in which to remove the fat from the intestines is by the use of calomel and the concoction, the recipe of which I have given. Work of course hardens the flesh, but it will not take the fat off except from the surface and the greatest care must be taken to prevent the fighters from becoming clogged, or to take cold while the medicine is in operation.

When the cocks are inclined to retain food in the craw it is either an indication that they are being fed too heavily or overworked, in which case I have found calves foot jelly to be a splendid, mild lavative.

The jelly is made by boiling, say 4 calves feet (from which the hair has been removed) until all the meat or gum leaves the bone and hoofs, then

skim, and pour into plates and allow
it to cool, when it will be transparent
and spongy like gelatine. Give each
cock half an ounce once a day until
the digestive organs properly perform
their functions. It will be best to
give them the jelly at noon as cocks
are more apt to retain food from dinner to supper than from breakfast to
dinner. I frequently give them a few
bites of apple, a little green plantain
or a few worms, all of which allays
fever and aids digestion.

The real hard work of the trainer
now starts. He must have the cocks
fed, weighed and worked, and the
coops cleaned by 7 a. m.

The cocks should be given no solid
food during the first four days of their
confinement. The oat and corn bread
is easily digested, and being made of
the most strengthening ingredients,
it is absolutely the best food that
they could have. I use the bread all
through the process of training, mix-
ing the corn and oat bread in equal
parts then adding ten pounds of
chipped oats, after being thoroughly

washed and dried. I give it to them
for breakfast and dinner, gradually
increasing the amount from one tablespoonful to all they can eat and digest.

It may be well to state the effect
which it has upon them. In the first
place it is strengthening, easily digested, and makes them "corky," i. e.
they tighten up, and when in the
hands they feel light and hard. All
other solid food has a tendency to
make them leady, and the fat hard to
keep down, besides the dead weight
which they carry makes them tire
easily in work and battle. Cracked
instead of whole corn is recommended
because it is not a fat producer, and
should be hand made instead of mill
ground, as by the latter process it is
ground too finely, making it hard for
them to digest.

It should be washed of all meal
and dried by the sun. Manufactured
hominy should never be used for
training fighting cocks, as it contains
lye, which is injurious to cocks while
being trained for battle.

THE WORK.

On about the fifth or sixth day you can start them to work. It is best to begin at night, as they can then have more time in which to rest. Make a cushion of hay, straw or other soft substance to work them on. The mat should be about 6 feet long, 3 feet wide and the height which will best suit the trainer. Begin with hand flirting, throwing them up twelve or fifteen times. Only the intelligence of the feeder can determine the proper way in which to handle them.

The fingers should never be closed tightly on the cock. They should be held straight, with the thumbs across the cock's back, and when the cock is raised to the level of the handler's face, the thumbs should be pressed downward quickly, thus causing the cock to spread his wings and throw out his legs, which exercises all parts of the body. On about the seventh or eighth day the cocks are strong enough to box. This should be done between breakfast and dinner, The muffs or gloves should be small and well filled, i. e., they should not be soft enough to allow the stubs of the spurs to be felt, and not hard enough to injure the cocks. They should be firmly tied on, and the cocks should be boxed or sparred on a large mat, or if that is not obtainable, straw will answer. The cocks should ₁not be allowed to box when they become fatigued. A few rounds of rapid work will suffice. On account of the impediments on the cocks' leg and the poor footing it is almost impossible to accurately judge a cock's real ability. As it is more like real fighting than any other exercise, the feeder can judge of the condition of the wind, which is an all important factor in cock fighting.

The trainer by this time can form a fair estimate of the condition of the cocks. He should give them all the hard food they can digest between meals, and all the work they can stand, though, he only can be the judge as to the amount of the food and work they should have.

What is meant by hard food is cracked corn, oats, and occasionally a feed of whole corn. About the eighth day they should be given about one-fourth of the white of a hard-boiled egg; chopped fine, with cracked corn. A few drops of tincture of iron, say twenty drops to a coop of thirty cocks, should be given occasionally in their drinking water. It is an excellent appetizer. It is prepared by dropping it into about a quart of water. Let each cock have three or four swallows three times a day.

The cocks' legs and head must be wiped every day and fresh straw put into the coops. They should be placed in sun coops out on the ground if the weather is not too cold, but care should be taken that they do not fill up on gravel or soil. When they are inclined to eat dirt it is an indication that they are feverish, and should be given a few drops of spirits of nitre, twenty drops to thirty cocks, in water and repeated until the fever subsides.

Hand rubbing is excellent for them,

it makes the flesh firm and stimulates a healthy flow of blood. There is no rule that a feeder can follow from day to day. He must be guided by intelligence. Some cocks will eat one kind of food, and others will not touch it.

How much fat a cock may lose can only be determined by the feeder, but it is safe to say cocks, if in good health, will not lose too much if properly fed and worked. It does not hurt them to spar two or three times during the course of training. If a cock loses appetite, let up on his work. If they have some feed in them at meal time, give them a little food and a few dips of water and let them remain in the sun coops as long as they are active.

They should be allowed to rest an honr after breakfast and dinner.

That is, the room should be darkened and they will sit down.

I believe in adhering as closely as possible to the laws of nature, but with game or fighting cocks it is different from the conditioning of fighting dogs, race horses or pugilists. It is not the nature of a cock to run or to be flirted in the air, or to be fed on artificial food, or to be cleaned out with drugs, yet all of this is necessary to the proper conditioning of fighting cocks. Every cocker has his own ideas about the business and naturally thinks them best. I have long since arrived at the conclusion that no one has a monopoly on knowledge pertaining to game cocks. I have spent fifty years of my life feeding, caring for and fighting game cocks. I have had no other pursuit in life; and even today as I sit at my cottage door watching my pets, as the sun dies away in the western sky, I can learn something new.

I shall not attempt to give any remedies for diseases which fighting cocks are heir to. The feeding house should not be a detention camp. It is impossible to get sick cocks into condition to fight. Throw them out on a good walk, and they may come around all right.

Cocks frequently take cold during

the process of training.; My only
remedy has been quinine, two grains
every night until cured. Keep the
bowels open, and it wil. soon pass off.
Cocks seldom lose their appetite from
that cause consequently their strength
is not impaired.

The food should be clean and dry
at all times, and if the feeder so de-
sires he can moisten it with beef tea,
but so long as the cocks eat and digest their food it is best for them. A
great many successful cockers advo-
cate the use of raw meat. I have used
it and found no benefit in it, as they
usually wind up with dysentery,
which is the most hurtful of all ailments.

THE CONDITION.

While it is almost impossible to
follow any rule as to feed and work
in training a main of cocks to fight
as some of the fowl may stand twice
as much work as others, and inci-
dentally a greater quantity of food.
Some will be feverish, some harder
to reduce in weight than others, some

become too thin, some may not eat at
all. Such is the experience of most
cockers, but we must do everything
as near systematically as consistent,
and while the following is but a rep-
etition of the former discourse on the
subject, it places the trainer's work
before him in a tabulated form.

FIRST DAY.

The cocks should all be cleaned of
mites by rubbing a little kerosene
around the vent and under the wings
and wherever the parasites are found;
the spurs sawed off; the tips of the
flight feathers cut off about half an
inch (it allows the oil to ooze out thus
making the feathers stiff,) and the
feathers cut from under the vent.
They should be given four or five dips
of water at night, and on the morning of the

SECOND DAY

they should be given the physic, and
half an hour or so after, each cock
should be given a tablespoonful of
sweetened water, the directions as to
the manner in which it is prepared

being given in the early pages. The
coops must be kept clean, the cocks
kept dry and no draught in the room
either in winter or summer. At noon
they can be given a little of the toast
bread, from which the water used after physicing is made. It should be
luke warm and very moist. Toward
evening or ab ut sundown, fresh
clean straw should be put into the
coops, and each cock given a tablespoonful of corn meal mush and sweet
milk, and on the morning of the

THIRD DAY

after w ighing the cocks and washing
their feet in warm water—they must
be weighed every morning–should be
given a tablespoonful of corn bread,
moistened with Leibig's Extract of
Beef, which should be milk warm.
The t er should take notice of the
effect the purgative has had upon the
different cocks; the amount of fat
they have lost, and those which have
lost th t weight should be kept
on s at least one day longer
than others, and his work should

also start one day later. It will be found that cocks that have been walked around pig pens or fed on soft food will lose more fat than those which have been corn fed. They are not naturally as strong as the well fed fellows and are harder to put in condition. At noon they should have a small feed of warm stale bread, moistened with water and allowed to remain quiet until evening when their beds can be made up and their feet cleaned, should they need it, and for supper each cock should have the same as the morning meal. On the morning of the

FOURTH DAY

they should be given a spoon____ of the bread (corn and oat,) dry, and half an hour or so after they should have three or four di____arley water. At noon the s____ with the barley, that is, ab____ half a teaspoonful of the cooked barley from which the water was ma____ for the morning drink. At nigh____ them all a tablespoonful of the ____ and oat bread (mixed as for the morning meal) and when they have finished eating give them three or four dips of pure water, fix the beds up nicely and on the morning of the

FIFTH DAY

you will find them feeling better than at any time during the process through which they have passed. All those that have been hearty and digested their food should have in addition to the corn and oat bread a le cracked corn—a teaspoonful— mixed with the bread. The others should have the bread, moistened with beef tea, and after the meal three our dips of water containing a few ops of tincture of iron. The cocks that have been given the cracked corn with the bread should be give or four dips of pure water. t noon give them all some of the bread and a bite of apple and a dip of pure water. At night give them all a feed of cracked corn and one-fourt the white of a hard boiled c and three or four dips of water. the morning of the

SIXTH DAY

examine each cock as they are being weighed and see if there is any food in the craw, marking the coops of those that are empty and of those that have not digested their food. The empty ones can have a feed of the bread, with a little oats and cracked corn mixed, and the others some of the calves foot jelly and two or three dips of beef tea. If they are empty at noon give them a feed of the corn bread, with a teaspoonful of oats. The cocks that were empty for breakfast should have a feed of the bread, with oats and cracked corn mixed. For the noon meal the feed should be a light one as they should be empty when the work begins. The cocks should be set out on the ground in sun coops for a few minutes if the weather permits, or if you leave some in doors it will be well to set them in ground coops, with plenty of fresh straw to scratch in. They exercise better when they have more room for action. The working mat should be

out of sight of the cocks in the coops
as they become excited with the flap-
ping of wings, etc. The cocks that
have eaten and digested their food
best will naturally stand more work
than the delicate ones, consequently,
if you start them off with fifteen
"flirts," as the tossing is called, give
the celicate fellows about ten flirts,
rub them all lightly down the back,
the breast, legs and under the wings,
keeping them at all times in a natural position while being rubbed.
While flirting see that they alight on
their feet. Don't handle them roughly at any time, and after a few days'
work they will seem to like it. For
supper give them all a feed of cracked
corn and one-fourth of the white of a
hard boiled egg, apportioning the
amount according to the appetite and
digestive power of the cock. Wind
up the day's work by giving each
cock a few dips of pure water. They
should always be allowed to rest at
least half an hour before being fed.

SEVENTH DAY.

   The work should be slightly increased, say from five to ten flirts more than last night and of course a gradual increase in the amount of food—that is, if they digest it properly; if not, feed and work th_m sparingly. The idea is not to allow them to become "clogged" that is, holding the food in the craw instead of digesting it. Those that are empty shoul1 have a heaping tablespoonful of cracked corn and oats mixed (not a tablespoonful of each,) and those retaining food should be given a small feed of corn bread with one-fourth of the white of a hard boiled egg chopped fine and mixed with the bread. Half an hour or so after breakfast let them have three or four dips of pure water and place them in coops on the ground if the weather permits; if not try to let them run in coops inside. The exercise helps them to digest their food. At noon give them the corn and oat bread mixed if they are empty. If not mix half a teaspoonful of boiled barley with it, and half an hour afterwards give them two or three dips of pure water. At night the work should be increased to, say thirty-five or forty flirts, and let them rest half an hour or so before feeding. They should all have cracked corn and the white of a hard boiled egg for supper. And as before, giving those that are empty the largest feed.

EIGHTH DAY.

There will be no change in the bill of fare or work, except to increase or decrease according to the condition of the cocks. They should not be overworked or overfed at any time, and only the intelligence of the feeder can determine what is best for them—that is, the amount of food and work which they should have. It is best that they should have solid food as long as they digest it, but when occasion requires it must be moistened, though it is not as good for them as the dry, solid food.

The white of hard boiled egg has been recognized by cockers from time immemorial as one of the best aids to the digestive organs, and it should be given to the cocks at least once each

day after they have been started to
work and put on hard food.

Tincture of iron acts as a stimulant
and creates an appetite and should be
given occasionally in water, say from
·15 to 25 drops in a quart of water,
allowing each cock from two to four
dips. Calves foot jelly is a mild lax-
ative, besides being soothing to the
bowels.

·Sweet spirits of nitre is somet·m s
used when cocks are feverish. Ten
to fifteen drops in a quart of water,
allowing the cocks to have from two
to four dips after eating. It is not
necessary to review the effect the different foods used have upon the
cocks. Suffice to say the strengthening properties contained in them, besides not being of a fat producing
nature, combine to make the best
that I have found for the purpose of
cond·tioning fighting-cocks.

Part II.

Rules of the Cock Pit.

Indianapolis Rules.

1. The two pitters shall choose a time-keeper and a referee. It shall be the duty of the former to keep time between rounds, and notify the handlers to "get ready" at twenty-five seconds, then call "time" at thirty seconds. The referee shall pay close attention to the handlers and the birds, and see that the following rules are strictly adhered to:

2. All birds under 6-4, weighing within two ounces of each other, are matched, except stags and broken-bill and blinker cocks, which shall be allowed four ounces against sound

cocks. Sound cocks weighing 6-4 and upwards shall be fought as shake-bags and matched regardless of weight.

3. All gaffs shall be round from socket to point; no others will be allowed.

4. After the birds are heeled they shall be weighed by the referee, who will call out their respective weights. He shall also examine the birds' gaffs.

5. Upon entering the pit the handlers shall let the cocks peck each other three or four times; they shall then step to their respective scores, (which scores shall be four feet each way from the center,) set their birds squarely on their feet and instantly release them.

6. It is no fight unless a blow is struck while both cocks show.

7. It shall be unfair for a handler to touch either cock except as directed by the referee.

8. The referee shall order a handler to give his cock a wing when necessary, or turn a bird that is on its back. These directions may be given

or y when the cocks are not touching each other.

9. The referee shall call "handle" whenever a cock is fast in his antagonist, in himself or in the pit, (except during a court, in which case the birds are not to be handled until the end of the count,) also at the end of "counts" and "minutes," and at other times when necessary.

10. The handler of the gaffed cock shall draw the heels, catching the leg of his opponent's bird below the hock joint. The birds must not be raised from the pit floor until after the gaffs have been drawn.

11. Thirty seconds is the time allowed in all handlings, time to commence as soon as the cocks are lifted off the floor of the pit.

12. Between pittings it shall be fair for the pitters to wash their birds' heads, give refreshments, and help their cocks in any other way possible. but they must be ready to pit promptly on call of time.

13. As soon as one cock ceases fighting, the referee shall call to the

handler of the fighting cock, "Mr. A., count;" whereupon that handler shall count ten in an audible tone. After being handled the cocks shall be pitted again and so continue until three tens in all have been counted. After the third count and handle, the cocks are to be placed breast to breast on the center score, when the pitter having the count shall count twenty and the fight is ended in his favor.

14. The count can be broken only bv a peck or blow from the cock which is being counted out, or by the death of the cock having the count, or by that cock showing unmistakable evidence of running away, in which cases the referee shall call "count broken."

15. If the cocks should both cease fighting at the same time, or should refuse to meet at the beginning of a round, the referee shall call for one minute's time, at the expiration of which the cocks are to be handled and again pitted. If they refuse to meet after the second minute, they

are to be handled and pitted again, until the expiration of the third minute, and then they are to be handled and breasted on the center score. And if they still refuse to fight at the expiration of one minute, a fresh cock is to be brought to the pit. If one combatant shows fight and the other does not, the battle is given to the fighting cock. If both fight or both refuse, it is a drawn battle.

16.   If both cocks die, neither having the count, the longest liver wins. If the cock having the count is dying and the other cock wanting to run, the former wins the battle even though he die before the expiration of the count.

17.   The referee shall watch all movement of the fight and confine the handlers strictly to the above rules. He may overlook what he believes to be an unintentional error, but must decide the battle against any handler who plainly and wilfully violates the rules.

New York Rules.

1. The pit shall be circular in shape, at least eighteen feet in diameter and not less than sixteen inches in height. The floor shall be covered with carpet or some other soft material. There shall be a chalk or some other mark made as near to the center of the pit as possible. There shall also be two outer marks which shall be one foot each way from the center mark.

2. Each pitter shall select a judge who shall select a referee. Said judges shall decide all matters in dispute during the pendency of the fight, but in case of their inability to agree, then it shall be the duty of the referee to decide and his decision shall be final.

3. Chickens shall take their age from the first day of March and sha'l be chickens during the fighting season.

4. It shall be deemed foul for any of the respective pitters to pit a bird with what is termed a foul hackle, that is, any of the feathers left whole

on the mane or neck.

5.   The pitter shall let each cock
bill the other three or more times,
but this is not to be construed that
the pitter of a cock has a right to bill
with his opponent's bird for the purpose of fatiguing him.

6.   No person shall be permitted
to handle his fowl after he is fairly
delivered in the pit, unless he counts
ten clear and distinct, without either
cock showing fight, or shall be fast
in his adversary, or fast in the carpet
or hung in the web of the pit, or in
himself.

7.   Any bird that may get on his
back shall be righted again by his
pi'ter, but not taken off the ground
he is lying on.

8.   Whenever a bird is fast in his
adversary the pitter of the cock the
spurs are fast in shall draw them out,
but the pitter of the cock has no
right to draw out his own spurs except when fast in himself, or in the
carpet or in the web of the pit.

9.   When either pitter has counted
ten tells successively without the cock

refusing fight, or making fight, or on the two cocks being again breasted fair on their fee , beak to beak on the center score, the cock refusing to fight shall be declared the loser on ten being counted. The pitters are bound to tell each ten as they count them; once. twice, etc.

10. No pitter, after the birds have been declared in the pit, shall be permitted to clean their beaks or eyes by blowing or otherwise, or be permitted to squeeze his fowl or press him against the floor during the pendency of the fight.

11. When a cock is pounded and no person takes it until the pitter counts twenty, and then counts nineteen or twenty and calls three times, "who takes it," and no person takes it, it is a battle to the cock the odds are on; but the pitter of the pounded cock has no right to have the pound put up, that is, $20 against $1. If this is not complied with the pitter shall go on as though there was no pourdage.

12. If a cock is pounded and the

poundage is taken, and if the cock
the odds are paid against should get
up and knock down his adversary,
then if the other bird is pounded and
the other poundage not taken before
the pitter counts twenty twice, and
calls out, "who takes it," three
times, he wins, although there was a
poundage before.

13. It shall be the duty of the respective pitters to deliver their bird
fair on the outer score or mark facing each other, and in a standing position, except on the fifth ten being
told, when the two birds shall be
placed on the center score, breast to
breast and beak to beak in like manner. Any pitter being guilty of
shoving his foot across the score, or
of pinching or using any other unfair
means for the purpose of making his
bird fight, shall lose the fight.

14. If both cocks fight together,
and then both should refuse until
they are counted out, a fresh bird is
to be hoveled and brought into the
pit, and the pitters are to toss for
which bird is to set to first. He that

wins has the choice. Then the one which is to set to last is to be taken up but not carried out of the pit. The hoveled bird is then to be put down to the other and allowed to fight while the judges or one of them shall count twenty. The same operation shall be gone through with the other bird and if one fight and the other refuse, it is a battle to the fighting cock, but if both fight or both refuse, it is a drawn battle.

15. If both birds refuse fighting until four, five, or more or less tens are counted, the pitter shall continue their count until one bird has refused ten times, for, when a pitter begins to count he counts for both cocks.

16. If a bird should die before he is counted out he wins the battle if he fights last. This, however, is not to apply when his adversary is running away.

17. The crowing or raising of the hackle is not fight, nor is fighting at the pitter's hands.

18. A breaking bird is a fighting bird, but a bird breaking from his ad-

versary is not fight.

19. If any dispute arises among
the pitters on the result of the fight
the birds are not to be taken from the
pit, nor the gaffs taken off until a decision has been made by the judges
or referee.

20. Each bird within two ounces
of each other shall be a match, except blinkers when they are fighting
against two eyed birds. An allowance from three to five ounces shall
be made. When blinkers are matched
they match even.

21. All matches must be fought
with heels, round from the socket to
the point, not to exceed one and a
quarter inches in length unless otherwise agreed upon. Drop Sockets,
Cutters, Slashers and twisted heels
shall be considered foul.

22. Previous to heeling cocks in
fighting mains the four spurs of same
pattern and size shall be placed together and the pitters shall toss for
choice of them.

23. In all mains at the end of
each battle, the judges shall order

the spurs to be changed, i. e., the spurs of the winning cock must be placed on the loser's next fowl and changed at the end of every battle.

24. Any person fighting a cock heavier than he is represented on the match list shall lose the fight, although he may have won.

25. In all cases of appeal, fighting ceases until the judges or referee gives their decision, which shall be final and strictly to the question before them.

26. When a bet is made it cannot be declared off unless by consent of both parties, all outside bets to go according to the main bet.

27. Each pitter, when delivering his bird on the score, shall take his hands off him as quickly as possible.

28. Any person violating any of the above rules shall be deemed to have lost the match.

New Orleans Rules.

1. All birds shall be weighed; give or take two ounces shall be a match, or otherwise it parties see fit to make it so.

2. All heels shall be round from socket to point or as nearly as possible.

3. When a stag is matched against a cock the stag will be entitled to four ounces advance in weight.

4. It shall be fair for handlers to pull feathers and sling blood or any other thing to help the bird between handlings.

5. It shall be foul for A or B to touch their birds while fighting unless one is fast to the other, but if a bird should unfortunately fasten himself with his own heel, it shall be fair to handle, but on no other consideration; and either handler violating or d.viating from the above rule shall lose his fight.

6. Thirty seconds shall be allowed between each and every round.

7. In counting, the bird showing fight last is entitled to the count, but

if his handler refuses to take the count the opposite handler shall be entitled to it.

8. The handler having the count shall pit his bird in his respective place when time is called and count ten and handle three more successive times. When time is called again the birds shall be placed in the center of the pit breast to breast and forty more counted, and if the bird not having the count refuses to fight, the one having it shall win.

9. A peck or blow at his opponent's bird and not at his handler will be considered fighting.

10. When time is called the handlers must let go their birds from their respective places fair and square; it shall be foul for either handler to pitch or toss his bird upon his opponent's, and either one violating this rule shall lose the fight.

11. Each party shall choose a judge and the judges choose a disinterested party as referee. No referee will be competent who has bet on either side, or is otherwise interested,

12. It shall be the duty of the referee and judges to watch all movements of the fight and judge according to the above rules. The referee will be confined to the opinions of the judges and his decision is final.

13. It shall be the duty of the referee to keep time between the rounds and notify the handlers to get ready at twenty-five seconds, then he must call time at thirty seconds when the handlers must be prompt in pitting their birds, and if either handler refuse to do so, he loses his fight.

Mobile Rules.

1. All cocks to be weighed and matched within two ounces of each other.

2. Cocks to be trimmed fairly; the shining feathers cut off their necks.

3. Cocks are to be fought with fair gaffs; all round points and blades are fair; flat points and sharp edges are unfair. The gaffs to be examined on entering the pit before the fight, by their respective pitters.

4.   If the pitters should forfeit th :
fight by acting contrary to the rules,
after the fight has commenced, then
by-bets are also forfeited.

5.   The pitters shall let the cocks
peck each other four or five times before they put them down, and place
them fairly on their feet without
pitching or throwing them toward
the opponent cock.

6.   The cocks are to be pitted five
or six feet apart, as long as they will
meet each other; when they refuse,
then the watch will be called; the
first time three minutes before they
are handled, and afterwards only one
minute is allowed for three pits, and
then they are to be pitted beak to
beak until the fight is ende l.

7.   In case neither cock fight in
five pits, then a mantle or fresh cock
must be brought into the pit to peck
both cocks; in case both cocks fight
it is a drawn battle, in case neither
cock fights it is also drawn.   If one
cock fights and the other refuse or
cannot fight, the fighting cock wins
the battle.   Neither cock is to be

taken out of the pit until the fresh
cock is brought in, and then a toss-up
which cock shall be tried first. No
refreshments to be given either cock
until after tried.

8. The pitter has a right to press
up his cock's legs and fix his wing
feathers in their proper places and
then walk deliberately to his score
and put his cock down, or when
called upon by his opponent pitter.

9. If one cock makes fight and the
other does not, the fighting cock
takes the count and counts ten, and
so on at every pit until he counts
forty; and if the cock still refuses to
fight they are pitted breast to breast
and then the pitter counts twenty,
which ends the fight in his favor.

10. The pitter must handle his
cock when hung in the other cock or
otherwise, and has a right to give
his cock a wing or turn him when on
his back, providing he does not touch
him. Drawing feathers from the
head, beak or eyes is allowed.

11. If one cock dies in the pit the
living cock wins the fight. If there

is a doubt of it being the cock matched, they have a right to weigh him after he is heeled. Every man forfeits the battle by refusing to weigh his cock.

12. If one pitter should make an attempt to handle his cock, and he should not be hung, then the other pitter has a right to handle his cock. Each pitter must stand three feet from the cocks while they are fighting.

13. It shall be at the option of the pitters or parties making the battle, to select each, one judge, to see that the above rules are observed; their decision, or that of the umpire to be chosen by them in case they disagree, to be final.

———

Hogan's Alley Rules.

1. All birds shall be weighed; give or take two ounces shall be a match, or otherwise if parties see fit to make it so.

2. In all mains, it is a matter of agreement as to time of weighing in, but in all hack fights, cocks must be

weighed in at ringside before the
public, and then each cock must be
held up in center of pit and weight
announced, thereby giving spectators
time to make their bets whilst cocks
are being heeled.

3. The pitters shall first present
their cocks beak to beak and either
cock refusing to show fight, the battle and all bets are declared off.

4. All heels to be fought shall be
round from socket to point, or as near
so as possible.

5. All stags shall be entitled to
four or six ounces when pitted against
a cock.

6. It shall be fair for handlers to
pull feathers out and sling blood, or
any other thing to help the bird between handling.

7. It shall be foul for A or B to
touch their birds while fighting, unless one is fast to the other; but if a
bird should unfortunately fasten himself with his own heel, it shall be
fair to handle but on no other consideration, and either handler violating the above rule, or in any way de-

viating from it, shall lose the fight.

8. Thirty seconds shall be allowed between each and every round.

9. In counting, the bird showing fight last shall be entitled to the count; but if his handler refuses to take the count, the opposite handler shall be entitled to it.

10. The handler having the count shall pit his bird in his respective place when time is called, and count ten and handle three or more successive times. When time is called again the birds shall be placed in the center of the pit, breast to breast, and twenty more be counted, and if the bird not having the count refuses to fight, the one having it shall be declared the winner. All counting must be done deliberately.

11. A peck or blow at his opponent's bird, and not at his handler, will be considered fighting.

12. When time is called the handlers must let go their birds from their respective places on the score line, fair and square; it shall be foul for either handler to pitch or toss his

bird upon his opponent's, and either one violating this rule shall lose the fight.

13. Each party shall choose a judge, and the judges choose a disinterested party as referee. No referee will be competent who has a bet on either side, or is otherwise interested.

14. It shall be the duty of the judges and referee to watch all movements of the fight and judge according to the above rule. The referee will be confined to the opinions of the judges only, and his decision is final.

15. It shall be the duty of the referee to keep time between the rounds and notify the handlers to "get ready" at twenty-five seconds; then he must call "time" at thirty seconds when the handlers must be prompt in pitting their birds, and if either handler refuses to do so, he shall lose the fight.

16. In case the cocks fall apart or stop fighting, it shall be the privilege of either pitter to call on the referee for time, which shall be three min-

utes; at the expiration of which they
must handle their cocks, and pit them
from their respective positions.
Should the cocks again refuse, or fail
to fight, time must be called, which
shall be one minute, when the pitters
shall handle and pit as before.
Should they again refuse to fight
time must be as in the former case
one minute and the cocks are to be
handled and pitted; and if they still
refuse or fail to fight, time is to be
again called, and the birds handled
as described above. The cocks are
then to be pitted breast to breast. If
both cocks refuse or fail to figh⁺ the
battle is to be declared a draw.

17.   If both cocks fight after being
pitted breast to breat and again fall
apart, they shall be breasted again
by their respective pitters. If both
cocks refuse to show or fail to fight,
the battle shall be given to the cock
last showing the fight.

18.   In all cases the battle is to be
given to the living cock, unless the
living cock be a runaway, in which
case the dead cock wins; to runaways

only, if both cocks die in the pit, the battle is to be given to the one living longest.

19. In all cases of dispute, or appeal by the pitters, the fighting ceases; birds are not to be taken from pit or gaffs taken off until a decision is rendered by the judges or the referee. Their decision shall be final and strictly to the question before them.

20. Any person fighting a bird different from the one represented on the match list in color or in weight shall lose the fight although his cock is victorious in the battle.

21. A cock who flies out of the pit from receiving a brain blow or any other case, there shall be allowed a reasonable time to have him caught a d brought back into the pit before time is called. Should his opponent d e before another pitting is had the living cock wins, but should he be p tted and again flies out of the pit, proving that he is a dunghill, the fight shall be given against him.

22. Shou d either of the handlers

be guilty of a slight error and the referee is satisfied that it was not intended he shall not give the battle against him, but warn him to offend no more. Should any doubt arise in the mind of the referee upon any question or point he shall take time to consider, that his decision will be found on the side of fair play and justice.

Garrigan Pit Rules.

1. All cocks and stags included to be matched and weighed in for Tournaments, Mains or Hack fights must be shown in full feather, but should any cock be shown that has previously been cut out in part or in whole his opponent can be cut out in like manner before weighing.

2. All sound cocks of equal weight or within two ounces of each other shall be a match, a one-eyed cock matched against a two-eyed cock shall have two ounces advance in weight, a one-eyed cock and a stag of equal weight give or take two

ounces shall be a match, a stag when matched against a sound cock shall have four ounces. A one-eyed stag when matched against a sound cock shall have eight ounces in weight, other weights will be matched only with the consent of the party having the lighter weight,

3.   All parties are allowed to use any set or length of gaffs that they may think their cocks will do the most execution with, provided they are round from point to socket. Chisel points or sword blade gaffs are foul and will not be allowed used.

4.   When cocks are heeled and ready for battle they must be re-weighed at the request of either pit-ter and should it be found that a heavier cock than the one shown and weighed for that battle was rung in, it shall be declared a rank fraud and the cock so rung in shall lose the battle without a blow being struck.

5.   A referee and time keeper shall be chosen that will be satisfatory to all parties concerned, or one may act in place of both, whose duty shall be

to keep time, to closely watch all
movements of the cocks and their
handlers during each battle, to see
that all cocks are fought upon their
merits, to enforce the rules and give
his decision in each case after due de-
liberation in strict accordance with
the question, the rules and justice,
and from his decision there shall be
no appeal.

6. A line shall be drawn in the
center of the pit, and not less than
four feet from this center line on each
side a score shall be made, each handler when pitting his cock must at all
times deliver him on his respective
score except when coming to a breast.

7. Thirty seconds will be allowed
between each and every round or pitting. Time to commence after the
pitters handle their cocks. In twenty-
five seconds the time keeper shall
notify the handlers to get ready and
in thirty seconds he shall order them
to pit their cocks. Should either
handler refuse to pit his cock when
crdered to do so he sha'l lose the
fight.

8. Handlers are allowed to examine the gaffs and cocks while held by each other before billing them. Should it be found that either cock had been greased, soaped, peppered or that any other substance had been put on his feathers to impede his oppenent's fighting, the party so offending shall not only lose the fight, but he shall be barred from further handling in the pit.

9. If all be found right and fair the handlers shall go to center line and bill their cocks. Should either cock refuse to snow fight the battle and all bets will be declared off. If both cocks show fight the handlers shall immediately step back and place their cocks on their respective score facing their handlers with one or both hands. Handlers will not be allowed at any time to push or shove their cocks toward their opponent and it will be foul for a handler to pitch or toss his cock on the other cock when breasting them.

10. Humane Rule. Handlers are allowed between each and every round

or pitting to clean, rub down, sponge and water their cocks, or assist and refresh them in any other way during the thirty seconds alloted.

11. It shall be foul for either handler to touch their cocks while fighting unless they are fast in each other, in themselves or in any part of the pit. A cock lying on his back can be turned on his breast by his handler if he so wishes or if the opposing handler demands it, providing his antagcnist is clear of him. A cock on his side or wing can be turned on his breast providing his opponent is clear of him, but in turning cocks over they must not be lifted from the pit.

12. Should the cocks fall apart and stop fighting or after being pitted they should refuse to come together and no one having the count the pitters shall call for time which shall be one minute, after which they must handle their cocks. After being pitted should they refuse to come together time will be called and one minute given when the handlers shall

handle and pit their cocks as before, after being pitted and time called for the third time and they still refuse to come together, the handlers shall pit them breast to breast. Should one cock fight and the other refuse while the pitter of the fighting cock counts twenty he shall lose the fight.

13. If both cocks fight when pitted breast to breast and again fall apart or get hung in each other the pitters shall handle in the regular way only they must continue to pit them breast to breast every thirty seconds until one is killed, counted out or the battle declared a draw, but should both cocks after being breasted refuse to fight a fresh cock shall be brought in and allowed to bill them. Should one fight and the other refuse, the battle will be given to the fighting cock but if both fight or both refuse, the fight will be a draw.

14. At any time during the fight should one cock stop fighting while the handler of the fighting cock counts ten he can handle his cock and claim the count, when they have been

pitted for three consecutive times and ten counted each time the handlers shall pit their cocks breast to breast and beak to beak and the handler having the count shall count twenty. Should the count not be broken before completed, the cock having the count wins.

15. No handler can force a count until one or both cocks stop fighting if one handler has the count and refuses to take it the other handler can claim it, should he so desire. Should a cock who has the count, die before he is breasted and the count completed, the fight shall be given to the living cock. Should both cocks die before the count is completed the longest liver wins. A living cock who is entitled to the count his handler shall keep on counting until the count is completed, which is three times ten and once twenty, and if the count is not broken before it is completed the cock that has the count wins the battle, although he should not make another peck or strike another blow after getting the count. The count

cannot be taken away from a cock who is justly entitled to it unless it be broken, and to break the count the opposing cock must show fight by either pecking or striking his opponent.

16. A cock who flies out of the pit from receiving a brain blow or any other cause there shall be allowed a reasonable time to have him caught and brought back into the pit before time is called. Should his opponent die before another pitting is had the living cock wins, but should he be pitted and again flies out of the pit, proving that he is a dunghill, the fight shall be given against him.

17. When a cock is on his back, side or wing, he cannot be touched if his opponent is standing on any part of him until time is called and the referee orders the cocks handled. Pitters can only pull gaffs out of their own cock and in doing so they must take hold of their opponent's cock below the knee.

18. In all cases of dispute arising between the pitters, or an appeal be-

ing made to the referee, the fighting shall cease, the cocks will not be taken from the pit nor shall the gaffs be taken off until the referee gives his decision. Any unfair handling or tricks resorted to by either handler shall be promptly forbidden by the referee and should the same unfair handling and tricks be continued after being so warned the fight shall be given against the offending party.

19. Should either of the handlers be guilty of a slight error and the referee is satisfied that it was not intended he shall not give the battle against him, but warn him to offend no more. Should any doubt arise in the mind of the referee upon any question or point he shall take time to consider, that his decision will be found on the side of fair play and justice.

Universal Pit Rules.

1. The size and shape of the pit is optional with these principles: the floor must be earth or turf three or

more inches deep. Two score marks shall be made therein; one three feet each way from the center of the pit.

2. Each handler shall choose a referee who in turn shall choose a Judge. One referee shall act as time-keeper and notify the handlers to get ready at twenty-five seconds and call time at thirty seconds.

3. The referees shall decide all battles and any dispute or claim of foul that may arise during the battle. But in case of their inability or failure to agree then the judge shall decide and his decision shall be final and binding to all concerned.

4. All cocks under six pounds, eight ounces, and weighing within two ounces of each other shall be considered a match (or otherwise if parties see fit to make it so) except when stags, broken bill and blinker cocks are matched against perfect cocks, in which case the stag or imperfect cock shall be entitled to four ounces advantage in weight. A stag and imperfect cock of equal weight are a match. All cocks weighing six

pounds, eight ounces and over shall
be fought as shakebags and matched
regardless of weight. Stags take
their age from the first day of March
and shall be declared cocks after the
first day of June the following year.

5. Gaffs with blades round from
the socket to the point and having
sockets with a straight face shall be
considered fair. Any handler bringing a cock in the pit heeled with any
other kind of heel forfeits the battle,
even though he may have won it.
Handlers may use their own judge-
ment in heeling.

6. All cocks shall be reweighed
after heeling at the pit side by the
referees who will call out their respective weights and see that they
conform with the match list. Any
handler showing other than he has
represented on the match list forfeits
the battle. The judge will cut the
heels off after each battle and see
that each wore fair heels.

7. Hackles must be fairly trimmed
not too long or too short. Handlers

(3)

may use their pleasure about cutting out the other parts of their cocks. If one cock is trimmed with a close unfair hack the referees shall order the other cut in the same manner.

8. Upon entering the pit the handlers will let their cocks peck each other several times, then they will step behind their respective scores and set their cocks cown behind their scores fairly on their feet and instantly release them at the word of the referee. Each cock must voluntarily go over his score. Each handler must remain behind his score until a blow is passed, and then they must not hover over their cocks but shall give them a chance to fight. It is no battle unless a blow is struck while both cocks show fight.

9. Thirty seconds are allowed for handling. During said thirty seconds handlers may nurse and refresh their cocks as they see fit, but each must pit his cock promptly on the call of time and if either fail or refuse to do so he loses the battle.

10. After the cocks have been

fairly delivered it shall be foul for either handler to touch his bird unless he counts ten clear and distinct while neither cock is fighting or touching the other unless he is fast. If he is fast in the pit or in himself he must be loosened by his handler, but if fast in his adversary, each handler shall at once lay hold of their respective cocks and the handler of the gaffed cock shall draw the heels, catching his opponents cock above the foot and below the knee. The cocks must not be lifted from the floor until the gaffs are drawn.

11. In counting, the cocks showing fight last shall be entitled to the count. Where-upon as soon as one cock ceases to fight the handler of the fighting cock will count ten and handle; he will then upon the call of time pit his cock behind his score and count ten more and handle and so continue until five tens are counted and after the fifth ten and handle, the cocks shall be brought to the center of the pit and pitted one foot apart(if either is blind they shall be

breasted,) and the handler having
the count will count twenty-five, and
if the count is not broken by the cock
the odds are on, the one having the
count shall be declared the winner.

12. The count can only be broken
by a peck or a blow from the cock
that is being counted out or by the
one having it running or wanting to
run, in which the count changes to
the other. If the cock having the
count gets fast in the other, the fifth
ten being told, no handle will be allowed until the end of the count, unless the other makes fight, and if the
other does make fight it renews the
counting from the first, and if he
fights last it is his count. A cock
pecking at any time when out of his
pitter's hands is fight, but pecking at
his handler's hands is not fight.

13. Should both cocks cease fighting at the same time, or refuse to
fight at the beginning of the round,
they shall be counted out both at
once, by the referee, and then a fresh
cock shall be brought in the pit and
allowed to fight each. If one fights

and the other refuses, the fighting cock win. If both fight or both refuse, it shall be declared a draw battle.

14. After a blow is passed while both cocks show and one runs away, he must be returned to the pit at once, and if he refuses to fight or leaves the pit the second time without striking a blow, he loses

---

Dead Bird Rules.

1. All birds shall be weighed before and after the fight, give or take two ounces shall be a match.

2. All stags shall be allowed four ounces when fighting against cocks.

3. All one-eyed cocks should be allowed four ounces when fighting against sound cocks. Blinker cocks against stags of even weight shall be a match.

4. All gaffs shall be round from socket to point, one and one-fourth (1¼) Regulation heel to be used unless otherwise agreed upon.

5. Coc's being ready and brought

into the pit, each pitter is to take his proper station and there remain until the gaffs are measured.

6.   The pitters shall present their cocks beak to beak and if either cock refuses to show fight all bets are off.

7.   If both cocks show fight each pitter shall step to his proper place and set their birds on the outer score and instantly release him. Either handler shoving his bird over the score loses the fight.

8.   The pitter whose cock may be fastened in his adversary shall steadily hold his cock while his opponent's pitter draws the heel or heels, and then instantly resume his original position and be in readiness to pit his cock when called by the time-keeper.

9.   All birds shall be pitted in full feather unless otherwise agreed upon.

10.   If a bird 's on his back his handler shall turn him over but not take him off the floor.

11.   If the birds stop fightiug the time-keeper shall order them breasted on the score.

12.   If either bird runs away he is

to be brought back twice and if refusing to fight the second time he loses the fight.

13. All cocks shall be fought until ceasing to show fight, be killed or run away.

14. Any pitter resorting to any act of trickery or attempt to assist his cock by other means than those prescribed in the above rules shall forfeit the fight.

California Pit Rules.

1. When the cocks are brought to the pit the pitters enter the same and no other persons shall be admitted within its limits. The pitters then proceed to examine the cocks and see that they have on fair heels. Secondly, that neither of the parties have resorted to the unmanly and foul practice of greasing, soaping, peppering or making any other external appliance, all of which are foul and inadmissible.

2. All things being right and fair the pitters shall deliver their cocks

fairly on their feet, upon the score and then retire one or two steps and not move their hands or walk around their cocks until a blow is struck. Then they may approach their cocks for the purpose of handling them when they hang. But they are not to hover over the cocks so as to retard or prevent them from making a blow. And if either cock refuses to make fight, it shall then be declared no match.

3. When the cocks are hung, the pitters shall lay hold of their respective cock and the party draws the heel, nor shall either party cause in any manner unnecessary injury or punishment while the heels are being extracted. As soon as the cocks are freed they shall again be delivered on the score.

4. All cocks hanged in the canvas, ground or in themselves shall be loosened by their respective pitters at all times.

5. When one or both cocks are hanged it is necessary to handle them and deliver them at the score so that

they may renew the combat fairly.

6. When the cocks are put to, if either cock refuses to fight, the other pitter has a right to count, when he proceeds. to count 40 deliberately, which when counted is not to be counted again during the battle.

7. Should either or both cocks after being delivered, not make fight, the pitter whose cock fought last shall be entitled to the count, when he shall count deliberately six times ten and at every count they shall both handle and deliver their cocks on the score. On the third and sixth count they shall deliver their cocks breast to breast, and if on the sixth count after being so delivered, they do not make fight, the pitter having the count shall have won the fight.

8. If in counting the law the other cock makes fight, that breaks the count, and if he is the last fighter he is entitled to the count. But one must neglect or refuse to make fight six successive times before the battle can be declared against him.

9. If either or both cocks die be-

fore the pitter finished counting the
law, the fight shall be awarded to the
last fighting cock.

10.   Neither pitter shall be allowed
to touch or handle his cock while
counting the law.

11.   No pitter shall be allowed to
suck or sling blood from his cock's
throat or mouth, nor pluck feathers
from over his eyes or out of his mouth.

12.   All cocks laying on their backs
shall be turned on their bellies, by
their respective pitters at all times,
provided the other cock is not standing on him.   If his pitter neglect or
refuse to turn him it is then admissible for the other pitter to turn him
gently on his belly.

13.   All cocks shall have a wing
given them, provided the other is not
upon it.   In giving the wing it is to
be placed gently by his side, without
raising the cock or helping him on
his feet.

14.   When both cocks break together and the pitters and judges are unable to decide which fought last or
when both are hanged in each other,

it shall be the duty of the judges to order them to the score Then if both refuse to fight the pitters shall count the law and have them put to, as if the count were actually going on and if neither make fight before the count is finished, the fight shall be pronounced a draw.

15. Any pitter acting contrary to the foregoing rules forfeits the battle.

Canadian Pit Rules.

1. The pit shall be at least twelve feet square and ten inches high with a chalk line across the center, running parallel with and three feet on either side of center chalk line, two outer lines must be drawn. The cocks must be pitted behind these outer lines.

2. All cocks shall be weighed, give or take two ounces being a match. When a stag is matched against a cock the stag is entitled to four ounces. When a blinker cock is matched against a two-eyed cock the blinker is entitled to four ounces.

A blinker cock and a stag of the same weight is a match.

3. When the cocks are fast it shall be fair to handle by me drawing your spurs out of my cock and you drawing my spurs out of your cock. The handlers are to give the birds room to fight and must not hover or press on them, each keeping on their respective sides of pit.

4. All heels to be fought with shall be round from socket to point. It shall be fair for handlers to pull feathers and sling blood or do anything to help the birds between handlings.

5. It shall be foul for A. or B. to touch their birds while fighting unless one is fast in the other, but if a bird should unfortunately fasten himself with his own heel it shall be fair to handle, but under no other consideration, and either handler violating or deviating from this rule shall lose the fight.

6. Thirty seconds shall be allowed between each and every round, twentyfive to get ready and five to pit.

7. In counting, the count shall be four tens and a forty. The bird showing fight last is entitled to the count but if his handler refuses to take the count, the opposite handler shall be entitled to it. The handler having the count shall pit his bird in his respective place when time is called then count ten and handle. This being repeated three more successive times and time being again called, the birds shall be placed breast to breast in the center of the pit with one hand and forty more counted. Then if the bird not having the count refuses to fight, the one having the count is declared winner.

8. A peck or blow at his opponent and not at his handler will be considered fighting. When time is called the handlers must let go of their birds from their respective places fairly and squarely. It shall be a foul for either handler to pitch and toss his bird, and either one violating these rules shall lose the fight.

9. Each party shall choose a judge and the judges choose a disin-

terested party as a referee. No person will be competent to act as referee who has bet on either side or is otherwise interested. It shall be the duty of the referee and judges to watch all movements of the fight and judge according to the above rules.

10. The referee will be confined to the opinion of the judges only and his decision shall be final. It is the duty of the referee to keep time between the rounds and notify the handlers to get ready at twenty-five seconds, calling time at thirty seconds when the handlers must be prompt in pitting their birds and if either handler refuses to do so he shall lose the fight.

11. If one cock is standing on another neither cock shall be touched while their feathers are touching. Wherefore if one cock is on his back his handler may turn him over or if his wing is away from him the handler may put the wing under him, but under no circumstances will he be allowed to put him on his feet.

National Pit Rules.

1. The pit shall be a circle as near as possible and not less than twelve feet in diameter and sixteen inches high. The floor shall be carpet, tan or some other suitable material. There shall be a chalk or other mark in the center of the pit, there shall also be two outer marks one foot each way from center mark.

2. Each pitter shall choose a judge who in turn shall choose a referee. Said judges shall decide all matters of dispute during the pending of the fight; but in case of their inability to agree then it shall be the duty of the referee to decide, and his decision shall be final.

3, All cocks shall be pitted in full feather except tail and wings which shall be cut unless otherwise mutually agreed upon by both parties making the fight.

4. The gaffs may be any length desired if round from point to socket, unless mutually agreed upon a certain length.

5. All cocks weighing within two

ounces of each other shall be a match
after the even and one weights are
matched; but if more matches can be
made by giving and taking two
ounces it is to be done.

6. All stags shall be allowed four
ounces when fighting against cocks,
also the same allowance will be given
to all one-eyed cocks when fighting
against sound birds.

7. It shall be the duty of the
referee to keep time between rounds.
Twenty-five seconds shall be allowed
to get ready and five seconds to pit,
when the handlers must be prompt in
pitting their cocks and if either handler refuses to do so, he shall lose the
fight.

8. All cocks shall be fought upon
their true merits, slight errors to be
overlooked. But if the same error be
repeated the pitter guilty of so doing
shall lose the fight.

9. Cocks ready and being brought
to the pit, each pitter shall take his
proper station and there remain until
the gaffs on the representative are
measured and examined by the respec-

tive judges and found to be in compliance with articles of agreement made. Regulating the length of gaffs in Rule 4.

10. The pitters shall first present their cocks beak to beak and either cock refusing to show fight the battle and all bets are declared off.

11. Both cocks showing, the pitters shall step to their respective positions in the pit and get their birds squarely on their feet and facing each other and instantly release them. Each pitter shall then return one or two paces back and there remain until one or both cocks shall be fastened, either in himself, the pit or his adversary. In either case he shall be allowed to handle his bird, and in no other case shall a pitter handle his cock except when he is down and it is necessary to give him a wing, then the pitter is to place the wing gently in its proper place and not to lift the cock. If a cock is on his back the pitter shall only be allowed to turn him over.

12. The pitter whose cock may be

hung in his adversary shall steadily hold his cock while the opposing handler draws the heel or heels, and instantly resume his original position and be in readiness to pit his cock when the time-keeper calls.

13. After each pitting the handlers shall be allowed to clean beaks and nurse their birds, but must be ready at the time designated in 7.

14. All cocks shall be fought until killed, run away or counted out. A run away shall immediately be brought and returned to the pit and instantly pitted; but in case either cock is down and unable to raise, they shall be breasted, then if either cock refuses to show after second breasting or pitting, said cock refusing shall be declared the loser.

15. At any time during the fight should one cock refuse or stop fighting the pitter of the cock showing fight shall count ten plainly and not hurry, the cocks are then to be handled and set again at the pitters' station, said pitter counting again and so repeat until four tens are counted

and naming the tens, 1, 2, 3, and 4, and immediately counting to twenty which shall give the battle to the cock having the count, unless the count shall be broken.

16. In case the cocks fall apart or stop fighting, it shall be the privilege of either pitter to call on the referee for time, which shall be three minutes; at the expiration of which they must handle their cocks, and pit them from their respective positions. Should the cocks again refuse, or fail to fight time must be called, which shall be one minute, when the pitters shall handle and pit as before. Should they again refuse to fight time must be as in the former case one minute and the cocks are to be handled and pitted; and if they still refuse or fail to fight, time is to be again called, and the birds handled as described above. The cocks are then to be pitted breast to breast. If both cocks refuse or fail to fight, the battle is to be declared a draw.

17. If both cocks fight after being pitted breast to breast and again fall

apart, they shall be breasted again by their respective pitters. If both cocks refuse to show, or fail to fight, the battle shall be given to the cock last showing fight.

18. In all cases the battle is to be given to the living cock, unless the living cock be a runaway, in which case the dead cock wins; to runaways only, if both cocks die in the pit, the battle is to be given to the one living longest.

19. In all cases of dispute, or appeal by the pitters, the fighting ceases; birds are not to be taken from pit or gaffs taken off until a decision is rendered by the judges or the referee. Their decision shall be final and strictly to the question before them.

20. Any person fighting a bird different from the one represented on the match list in color or in weight shall lose the fight although his cock is victorious in the battle.

21. It shall be the duty of the judges and referee to notice all movements of the fight and judge according to the above rules,

22. Any pitter caught in any act of trickery or attempt to aid his cock by other means than those prescribed by these rules shall lose the fight.

23. An interval of—minutes shall be allowed between the termination of one battle and the commencement of another.

24. Profane or boisterous language or any other unruly behavior will not be tolerated upon any occasion. And any person guilty of such act will be promptly ejected from the pit.

Colorado Pit Rules.

1. All birds weighing within two ounces of each other shall be a match.

2 When a stag is matched against a cock, the stag will be entitled to four ounces advantage in weight.

3. A blinker is allowed four ounces when he fights against a sound cock.

4. A sound stag and blinker cock are considered equal.

5. All birds to be shown with a long natural hackle.

6. All matches to be fought with

1½ inch club heels, unless otherwise agreed upon.

7.   All stags will fight as stags to the first of July.

8.   Each handler may have one attendent who will furnish him with any article he may require.

9.   In no case shall any person instruct or assist the handlers in the pit.

10.   It shall be fair for handlers to pull feathers and sling blood, or any other thing to help their birds between handlings.

11.   It shall be foul for A. or B. to touch their birds while fighting unless one is fast in the other.   But if a bird should fasten himself with his own heel, either in the pit or carpet, it shall be fair to handle but on no other consideration.   And either handler violating this rule shall lose his fight.

12.   In counting, the bird fighting last shall be entitled to the count. But if his handler refuses to take it, the opposite handler shall be entitled to it.

13.   The handler having the count

shall pit his bird in his respective place when time is called, and count ten, then handle three more successive times. When time is called again the birds shall be placed in the center of the pit, breast to breast, and forty more counted, and if the bird not having the count refuses to fight, the one having it shall be declared winner.

14. When time is called the handlers must let go their birds from their respective places, fair and square, for it shall be foul for either handler to pitch or toss his bird upon nis opponent. Either one violating the above rule shall lose the fight.

15. A peck at his opponent's bird and not at his handler will be considered fighting.

16. It shall be the duty of the referee to keep time between the rounds and notify the handlers to get ready at 25 seconds, then call time at 30 seconds. The handlers must be prompt in pitting their birds, and if either handler refuses to do so he shall lose the fight.

17. The pit shall be 18 feet in di-

ameter and 22 inches in height, a chalk mark in center and two outer marks five feet each way from center.

Ohio Pit Rules.

1.   The pit to be at least twelve feet in diameter, not less than sixteen inches in heighth and there shall be a chalk mark or other line made in the center of the pit; there shall also be two outer marks which shall be three feet each way from center line.

2.   All birds shall be weighed, give or take two ounces, shall be a match except when a blinker fights a strong fowl and then he shall be allowed four ounces. A stag shall be allowed four ounces when fighting against a cock.

3.   Fowls shall take their age from the first of March and shall be stags and pullets during the fighting season to-wit: From the first of March to the first day of June the following year.

4.   When fighting in main, the birds shall be weighed in full feather

and then to be weighed when brought to the pit by the referee, and either bird weighing more than called for on the list shall lose the fight.

5. The heels to be fair round blades from socket to the points and measured from point to top of thimble. Either party bringing a cock into the pit with longer or any other kind from that agreed, shall forfeit the fight.

6. If any dispute arises between the pitters on the result of the fight, the birds are not to be taken out of pit, nor the gaffs taken off until decided by the referee.

7. It shall be fair for handler to pull feathers and sling blood or anything to help his bird when in hand, except to take his heels off.

8. It shall be foul for A. or B. to touch the birds while fighting unless one is fast in himself or fast in the pit or his adversary. Both pitters are immediately to take hold of their respective cocks and the pitter whose cock is hung shall hold him steady while the adverse draws out the heel.

9. Fifteen seconds shall be allowed

between each and every round.

10. In counting, the bird showing fight last shall be entitled to the count, but if the handler refuses to take the count, the opposite handler shall be entitled to it.

11. The handler having the count shall pit his bird in his respective place when time is called, count ten, then handle three more successive times. When time is called again the birds shall be placed in the center of the pit, breast to breast and forty more counted and if the bird not having the count refuses to fight, the one having it shall be the winner.

12. In counting the last forty the birds are not to be handled unless the count is broken.

13. A peck or a blow at the opponent's bird and not at his handler, is considered fighting.

14. A cock when on his back shall be turned over on his belly by his pitter, with one hand.

15. When time is called the handlers must be prompt and let go their birds from their score, which is three

feet each way from the center mark and step back to his corner and there remain until the birds begin fighting. He shall stand two paces from the birds and not hover over them and refusing to do so, shall lose the fight.

16. A fighting cock can not break his own count.

17. Each shall choose a judge and the judges shall choose a disinterested party for a referee. No referee shall be competent who has bet on either side or is otherwise interested.

18. It shall be the duty of the judges and referee to watch all movements of the fight and judge according to the above rules. The referee will be confined to the opinion of the judges only and his decision final.

19. It shall be the duty of the referee to keep time between the rounds and notify the handlers to get ready at ten seconds and call time at fifteen seconds.

20. No one is allowed to handle or examine the cocks or his heels while in the pit except the pitters, referee and judge.

Spring City Pit Rules.

1.   The pit must be a ground floor unless otherwise agreed to and should be 16 or 18 feet in diameter.

2.   The cock or stag must be weighed in a bag. A stag fighting a cock has an allowance of 4 ounces in weight. A blinker cock fighting a two eyed one has four ounces. A blinker cock and a stag of one weight are a match. Give and take 2 ounces is a match.

3.   The cocks being weighed an l matched you will cut them out. You must cut the hackle with all the shiners off cr not at all. You can use your own pleasure about cutting out other parts of your cork or stag.

4.   Your cock being cut out you will heel him. You can heel him with paper and water, and nothing but that and flat on the leg. No bolstering or padding of heels allowed. If you do you will lose the battle ir the other parties find it out.

5.   Your cock being heeled you will bring him in the pit for battle, You will bill the cock, three times;

then you will stand apart 6 feet; then you will deliver your cock fair on his feet either to the right or left of your score for his battle.

6. In fighting, according to these rules, when you deliver your cock on his score you must stand back of him and not walk around him or lean over him to hide him from the other cock.

7. A cock breaking with another cock is fight, and a picking at any time on the ground is fight, but picking while in your hands is not fight. He must make fight after you have delivered him out of your hands.

8. When the cocks are fast you must handle by me drawing your spur out of my cock and you drawing my spur out of your cock. You then have thirty seconds to nurse your cock. The judge will call down cocks. Then you must strictly obey and put your cock down to renew the battle. In case one of the cocks gets disabled you can count him out. You can lay your cock down on his wing and count ten without the other cock making fight. Then you can handle him

again and so on until you count five
tens. Then you can get ready to
breast your cocks. You must put
them down on their feet and breast to
breast and if the crippled cock refuses
to fight while the opposite handler
counts twenty more, he has lost the
fight.

9. You are not bound to lay your
cock down on his wing. You can use
your own pleasure whether to lay him
on his wing or on his feet. If it is to
your advantage for your cock to fight
put him down on his feet and let him
fight.

10. In counting a cock out after
you have breasted them and you are
counting twenty if the cock should
get into the disabled cock you dare
not put your hands on them unless
the disabled cock makes fight, and if
he does you can handle, and by his
making fight it will renew all the
counting from the first and if the
disabled cock makes fight last it is
his count.

11. All cocks on their backs are to
be turned over on their bellies at all

times by his handlers, but not taken off the ground. Should he be hung in himself or canvass he is to be loosened, but not handled.

12. All heels to be round from socket to point. Drop sockets and slashers not allowed. The greasing, peppering, muffing and soaping a cock or any other external application will be deemed unfair and condemned. The application will be deemed unfair and condemned. The judges keep the time.

13. All bets go as main stakes. Any man not paying bets he lost will not be allowed to bet thereafter.

Maryland Pit Rules.

1. All cocks within two ounces of each other in weight shall be a match excepting blinkers and stags which shall be entitled to four ounces advance in weight when fighting two-eyed cocks.

2. All birds shall take their age from April 1st and shall fight as stags until April 2nd the following year.

3. All cocks or stags must have their shining hackle feathers cut off close before they are brought in the pit. The fact of a handler failing to do this before the bird is put on the scale, shall cause him to forfeit the battle on appeal from his opponent. except it be one or two feathers which shall not be sufficient to be claimed foul. The handler can please himself as to whether he cuts tail or wings.

4. All gaffs used under these rules must be round from socket to point, 1¼ or 1½ inches long from top of socket to point of blade. Drop Socket or Regulation, with or without flange, shall be allowed.

5. You can use paper or chamois skin for packing on the spur in heeling, but pillaring the leg above or below the spur shall be foul. Strings must be of light twine or wax end. When your bird is heeled you will bring him in the pit to be weighed, and if a bird is over the match weight more than two ounces, it shall be disqualified and ten minutes will be allowed to bring a different bird on

the scales at weight. No one shall be allowed to cut any feathers after the bird is scaled. Only one ten minutes and one substitute bird shall be allowed. The referee shall weigh all birds.

6. When birds are weighed and matched, the handlers shall take their side of the pit which shall be decided by the toss of a coin, and shall change sides each battle throughout. The referee shall order the handlers to bill their cocks in the center of the pit for a half minute. Then they shall take their position back of the score, which shall be six feet from the center score. The referee shall then order them to "down cocks" which must be done at once, on all orders from the referee at all times.

7. The cocks must be delivered on their score and not in front of it, straight across the pit and squarely on his feet, unless he is blinked or disabled, when his handler is allowed to put him down sideways or on his wing or breast.   (4)

8. When the handler delivers his bird on the pit, he must stand or kneel at his own score, and shall not follow his cock or hover around him in his fighting, he or they must keep well back from the cocks until the referee calls "handle cocks." then neither pitter shall be at liberty to handle if the cocks are hung in each other until both are prepared to lift their birds. *Provided.* That if a cock is hung in himself, or in the pit, or on his back; his handler is at liberty to loosen him or give him a wing, by turning him on his side. After first calling the judge's attention to the same.

9. Thirty seconds shall be allowed to nurse cocks between the pittings. The referee shall be official time-keeper, and shall do all calling to handlers in regard to the putting down or taking up of a cock; except when a cock is so disabled as to quit fighting. In such case the handler of the fighting cock can appeal to the judges for a "count out," and if no protest is made, he can count

twenty in s ccession and then lift his
cock.　Then when the required thirty
seconds have expired he can proceed
to count the disabled cock to a breast
by laying his cock down and then
count ten, then handle him a few seconds and lay him down, count and
handle as before, until ten has been
counted the third time, now the referee shall order the cocks breasted at
once, and if the non fighting cock
does not show fight while the opposite handler counts twenty he shall
lose the battle　But if he shows fight
it will renew all the counting.　If
both cocks come together in a buckle
and are disabled and either party
takes the count, then when they are
breasted and neither shows fight it
shall be a drawn battle.　When there
is a chance for a count, and the one
entitled does not take it, then his op-
p nent has that right.

　　10.　In case of a brained or running
cock, after he has left the pit twice,
his handler can demand his opponent
to bill him.　If he shows fight in b l-
in g an d rull e B ur be is pitted, then

he shall lose the battle. If a cock runs out and cannot be easily caught, the referee will allow time to catch him the first or second time.

11. Whenever cocks are fighting out of the pit they shall be handled without violating these rules. But any violation of these while the cocks are in the pit, will cost the loss of the fight.

12. The pit shall have a ground floor and be a smooth, level surface and should be 16 or 18 feet in diameter. Each handler shall be allowed a bottle holder. Two judges shall be chosen by the principals, one each, and they shall choose a referee. All appeals shall be made to the judges and upon their disagreeing the referee shall decide finally.

13. These rules shall govern the cock fighting in the western counties of the state of Maryland. And any person using foul means in connection with these rules shall lose all fights in which they are detected by officials.

14. The judges will cut all gaffs off after each fight. Judge A will

cut handler B's gaffs off. Twenty minutes will be allowed from the time gaffs are cut off until the next cock is brought in.

15. All choices must be determined by toss of coin. In fighting mains, they must fight in order from top to bottom weight or vice versa.

The Battle Royal.

1. Any number of cocks may be put in.

2. No limit as to age, condition or weight.

3. Use any kind of gaff all agree to.

4. Entry fee for each bird to be placed in stakeholder's hands before the fun begins.

5. All being in readiness, cocks arranged around the pit an equal distance apart, with heads touching cushion and tails toward center of pit, all must be liberated at the referee's call of "Go."

6. The referee. (or any other man chosen for the purpose) will draw

heels for all birds as fast as they get
hung, without changi ig position of
birds or helping them in any way.
With this exception the cocks are
not to be touched u itil a ''a i i.dls'' is
called.

7. Dead cocks shall be left in the
pit. An actual runner shall not be
returned.

8. The two remaining cocks are
to be fought according to rules gov-
erning mains in your cocking circle.

Boston Pit Rules.

1. All fowls brought to the pit
must be weighed and marked down,
for those to see that have fowls to
fight

2. Fowls within two ounces are a
match.

3. A stag is allowed four ounces
when he fights a cock.

4. A blinker is allowed four ounces
when he fights a sound fowl.

5. Fowls being ready, they are
brought into the pit.

6. Each man takes his station, and

sets his fowl to the right or · left, as he pleases, there remains till the fowls are in one another, or in the tan, or on his back,

7. The handler shall not assist his fowl from where he sits him, if he does, he forfeits the battle.

8. In no case shall they handle the fowls, unless they are in one another, or can count ten between fighting.

9. The fowls in hand, each man to his station; either counting ten, the fowls must be set, or the delinquent loses the match.

10. The fowls set, either refuses to show fight, the last that showed has the count, which is five times ten and then they are breasted.

11. The fowls are breasted at every five times ten, after once breasted.

12. The fowls brought to the breast, the one that had the count counts five times ten more, and then twenty; then he claims the battle, which is his.

13. In case the fowls show while counting, it destroys the count, and they commence again.

14. In case a fowl is on his back, his handler can turn him over.

15. In all cases the parties can select judges from the company present.

16. In case there are no judges, it will be left to the keeper of the pit.

17. In no cases shall any person talk with the handlers while the fowls are fighting.

18. All disorderly persons will be requested to leave immediately.

19. All weighing will be left to a man selected for the purpose.

20. All matches will be fought with round heels, unless otherwise agreed upon.

21. A man known to use any other, unless agreed upon, forfeits the battle.

22. All cutters, slashers and twisted heels are barred from this pit.

23. In all cases the last fowl that shows fight, has the count.

24. All fowls brought to the pit that do not show fight, do not lose the battle, unless otherwise agreed upon.

Philadelphia Pit Rules.

1.   The pit must be a ground floor unless otherwise agreed to.

2.   The cock or stag must be weighed enclosed in a small bag, and then two ounces deducted for the weight of the bag and feathers. A stag fighting a cock has an allowance of four ounces in weight; a blinker fighting a two-eyed bird has four ounces; a blinker cock and a stag of one weight are a match.

3.   The birds being weighed and matched, you must trim them out; cutting off all shiners on the hackle; you can use your own pleasure about cutting out other parts of your fowl.

4.   Your bird now being cut out you will heel him; you can use for packing nothing but paper and water; if you do you will lose the battle if the other party objects.

5.   Your bird being heeled you will bring him in the pit for battle; you will bill them one minute and then put them down behind their scores for battle.

6.   In fighting a battle, according

to these rul s, when you deliver your
f wl on his s re, you must stand
back of him and not le n ver him to
hide him from the other.

7. A cock breaking with an ther
cock is fight, and a cock picking at
any time when on the ground is fight;
but picking while in your hands is
not fight; he must make fight after
you deliver him out of your hands.

8. When the birds are fast you
must handle, by my drawing your
spur out of my fowl and you drawing
my spur out of your fowl; you then
have thirty seconds to nurse your
fowl; the judge will then call "down
cocks," and you must obey and put
your bird down to renew the battle.
In case one of the birds is disabled,
you can count him out; you can lay
your bird on his wing on his score,
and count ten without the other making fight; you can handle him again
and so on until you count five tens.
Then you get ready to breast your
birds. You must put them down on
their feet breast to breast. and if the
crippled cock refuses to fight while

the opposite handler counts twenty more, he has lost the battle.

9. You are not bound to lay your bird on his wing; you can use your pleasure whether you lay him on his wing or put him on his feet. If it is to your advantage for your bird to fight, put him on his feet and let him fight.

10. In counting a cock out, after you break them and are counting twenty, if the cock should get fast in the disabled one, you dare not put your hands on them unless the disabled bird makes fight; and if he does make fight you can handle, and by this making fight it will renew all the counting from the first; and if the disabled cock should make fight last it is his count.

11. The judges cut the heels off, and if all is right you must get ready for the next battle; you are allowed twenty minutes to be in the pit for the next battle. The judges are to keep the time.

12. All outside bets are to go as the main stakes. Any man not pay-

ing bets that he lost will not be allowed in any pit in Philadelphia thereafter.

Southern Pit Rules.

1.   When the cocks are in the pit the judges are to examine whether they are fairly trimmed and have fair heels. If all be right and fair the pitters are to deliver their cocks six feet apart (or thereabouts) and retire a step or two back; but if a wrong cock should be produced the party so offending forfeits the battle.

2.   All heels that are round from the socket to the point are allowed to be fair; any pitter bringing a cock into the pit with any other kind of heels, except by particular agreement, forfeits the battle.

3.   If either cock should be trimmed with a close, unfair back, the judge shall direct the other to be cut in the same manner, and at the time shall observe to the pitter that if he brings another cock in the like situation unless he shall have been previously trimmed, he shall forfeit the

battle.

4. A pitter when he delivers his cock shall retire two paces back, and not advance or walk around his cock until a blow has passed.

5. An interval of — minutes shall be allowed between the termination of one battle and the commencement of another.

6. No pitter shall pull a feather out of a cock's mouth or from over his eyes or head, or pluck him by the breast to make him fight, or punch him for the like purpose, under penalty of forfeiting the battle.

7. The pitters are to give the cocks room to fight, and are not to hover or press on them so as to retard their striking.

8. The greasing, peppering, muffing, and soaping a cock, or any other external application are unfair practices, and by no means admissible in this amusement.

9. The judges, when required, may suffer a pitter to call in some of his friends to assist in catching the cock, who are to retire immediately

when the cock is caught, and in no other instance is the judge to suffer the pit to be broken.

10. All cocks on their backs are to be immediately turned over on their bellies by their respective pitters at all times.

11. A cock when down is to have a wing given him if he needs it, unless his adversary is on it, but his pitter is to place the wing gently in its proper position, and not to lift the cock; and no wing is to be given unless absolutely necessary.

12. If either cock should be hung in himself, in the pit, or in the canvas, he is to be loosed by his pitter; but if in his adversary, both pitters are to immediately lay hold of their respective cocks, and the pitter whose cock is hung shall hold them steady while the adverse draws out the heel, and then they shall take their cocks asunder a sufficient distance for them fairly to renew the combat.

13. Should the cocks separate and the judges be unable to decide which fought last, he shall at his discretion

direct the pitters to carry their cocks
to the middle of the pit and deliver
them back to back, unless either of
them is blind; in that case they are
to be shouldered, that is, delivered
with their breasts touching, each pitter taking care to deliver his cock at
this, as well as at all times with one
hand.

14. When both cocks cease fighting it is then in the power of the pitter of the last fighting cock, unless
they touch each other, to demand a
count of the judges, who shall count
forty deliberately, which, when
counted out, is not to be counted
again during the battle. Then the
pitters shall catch their cocks and
carry them to the middle of the pit
and deliver them beak to beak; but to
be shouldered if either are blind as
before. Then if either cock refuses
or neglects to fight the judge shall
count ten, and shall direct the pitters
to bring their cocks again to the middle of the pit and pit as before; and
if the same cock in like manner refuses, he shall count ten again and

call out "twice refused," and so proceed until one cock thus refuses six
times successively. The judge shall
t'ien determine the battle against
such cock.

15. If either cock dies before the
judge can finish the counting of the
law, the battle is to be given to the
living cock, and if both die the longest liver wins the battle.

16. The pitters are not to touch
their cocks whilst the judge is in the
act of counting.

17. No pitter is ever to lay hold of
his adversary's cock, unless to draw
out the heel, and then he must take
him below the knee. Then there
shall be no second delivery, that is,
after he is once delivered he shall not
be touched until a blow is struck, unless ordered.

18. No pitter shall touch his cock
unless at the time mentioned in the
foregoing rules.

19. If any pitter acts contrary to
these rules the judge, if called upon
at the time, shall give the battle
against him.

Articles of Agreement.

We, the undersigned, do hereby agree, that on the——day of——, one thousand — hundred and——, will produce, show and weigh —— cocks (or stags,) between the weights of — and —, and to match all that weigh within two ounces of each other, and that the party's cocks that win the greatest number of battles shall be entitled to the sum of $——; the amount to be placed in the hands of Mr.——————, before any cocks are pitted. Be it further agreed that all cocks shall fight with fair heels, fair hackles. and to be subject to the —— rules in cock fighting, and that all profits arising from the spectators, called d or money, shall be——, after all charges are paid that usually happen on these occasions. Be it further agreed that the above named rules governing this main shall be considered as part of these articles and all provisions therein will govern any difficulty that may arise. Witness our hand, this the — day of —, 19—.

Signed,   —— ——

Witnesses:

Heeling, Handling, Etc.
A Word to the Wise.

While it has been our desire to compile a book of valuable information to the breeder and cocker (old and young) and while we are going to give you illustrations on heeling and the experience of some of our most noted cockers, we wish to state to the amateur in the beginning that to definite rule can be compiled for heeling and handling. A good heeler and handler is not to be despised by any man, but be sure that that man is yourself, heeling and handling your own birds. Condition your own birds, watch them closely, note how they fight, put the boxing gloves on and spar them. Take them to the pit, tie the heels on the way the natural spurs set, and turn them loose, and if they are fighters they will win a majority for you. I would rather have a good fighting cock heeled with horse shoe nails, than a poor fighter heeled with the best gaffs made.

Now for the handling—no special rule can be laid down by which all men can handle all birds. A good handler is a man who has had practical experience, and one who studies his birds and also his opponent's birds. To be a good pitter you must be a man of many resources—maintain the utmost co. posure, and not allow yourself to become excited by the remarks of the spectators or the opposite pitter. You must be thoroughly conversant with the rules of the pit, and strive for every advantage possible within the rules. More fights are won by the handling than the heeling. And remember that a leg fighter will cut with any length heel, or any set, and that a great fluttering cock is only a wing fighter and that your gaffs are not tied on the wings.

PUBLISHER.

A great many cockers try to impress upon the minds of the beginners that the art of heeling cocks properly belongs only to a few, and that the said old "fogie" is past grand master of

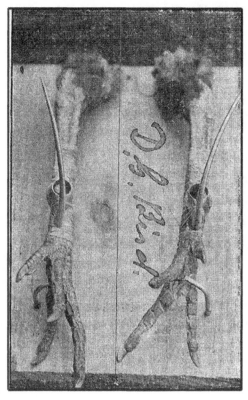

This is a popular way am ng our most successful cockers to set a 2 in. full drop socket regulation gaff.

the aforesaid art, and that when he dies there shall be no one sufficiently versed in the art to take his place. The gaffs should be of the very best quality of steel.

Have the cock properly held and do not put too much bolstering under the socket, as the farther the latter is from the leg the less force goes with the blow. Enough padding should be placed under the socket to prevent the cramping of the leg. The socket should be snugly fitted over the stub, using small pieces of kid, then use wax ends with which to tie them on. Make the spur set on firmly by drawing the string reasonably tight, using great care that they should be neither tight enough to cramp or loose enough to come off.

The points of long gaffs should be on a line with the outside of the hock, and short gaffs on a line with the middle of the leg, taking the cock's knee or hock as a guide. I have never found any one who could intelligently explain why the point of one spur was set outside and the other inside. When cocks "hang" themselves it is not the fault of the heeler but the cock.

When the cocks do good execution, it is the cocks not the heeler. Some cocks are "cutters" naturally, while gaff. are impediments to others. There is no way in which you can improve them, and I do n t know of a method by which to judge good cutters from the other kind. I have met cockers who have tried to explain it to me, but it was "theory," and in after years I found that they knew no more about it than I.

This is a successful way of setting a 1¼ inch full drop socket gaff.

Another Mode of Heeling.

Note what Mr. H. A. Piante, of Randall, N. Y., has to say of heeling.

"Now boys, you flatter the Heeler, and Handler very much when you claim he possesses knowledge you can not acquire yourself.

I never could discover any great amount of science in putting on a pair of gaffs; at least not so much, but I could give it all away in a moment. Now boys, if you think it's so much in heeling, just try some day, and heel a first class, good strong cock, in good condition against a so-called professional heeler, (cocks even in weight,) and heel your cock one heel about straight for the leader, and one just ahead of it, and see how much advantage the professional has in the battle.

I will guarantee he won't bet you to a stand-still, just because you never tied on a pair of gaffs; it's the cock they will be afraid of after you let him go, and although they have an idea your cock is not heeled exactly as they would do it, *they will tremble in their shoes*—when he strikes.

Now boys, learn to heel and handle your own fowl, and enjoy all the sport there is in it."

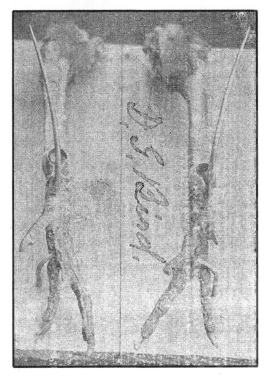

This cut represents a 3 inch gaff properly set.

All of our most successful breeders and cockers and noted heelers and handlers quote from J. W. Cooper on

This cut shows how to set a 2¼ in. full drop socket regulation gaff.

---

this subject, who advises as follows: "Let your fowl be held so that the inside of the leg will be perfectly level, then take your thumb and fore finger and work the back toe of the fowl. While doing this you will see

the leader of the leg rise and fall at
the upper joint. You will set the
right gaff on a line with the outside
of the leader at the upper joint of the
leg, and the left gaff you will set on
a line with the outside of the leader
at the upper joint."

This is for 1¼ inch gaff, and if
you are using a longer gaff and setting according to this rule, you must
do your sighting at 1¼ inch up the
gaff. Knowing that as the gaff is
longer it will be swinging out farther,
according to length. But this is the
rule by which all gaffs are set; re-
membering that at the same length
they have the same set, but as the
gaffs get longer they show to be
farther out at the point.

Trimming.

The *flight* feathers should be trimmed as far down as they are *limber*,
and the outside cut to be the same
length as the longest flight feathers.
The saddle feathers should be trimmed
in such a manner as not to im-

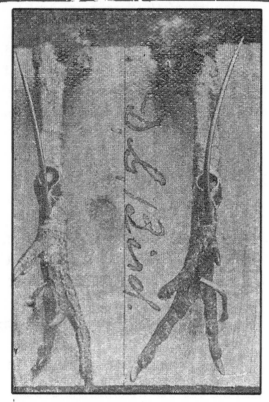

The above cut shows as near as we can tell you a popular way to set a 2½ full drop socket gaff.

pede the action of the wing. The tail should not be cut *short* as it makes a cock awkward in fighting, and acts as a balance while the cock is in the act of striking. The hackle should

be trimmed so as to allow the feathers
nearest the shoulders to form a mantle—that is, only cut off the shining
part of the plumage. It matters not
how close the feathers are cut from
around the neck close to the head.
The feathers which are on the outside
of the thighs should be cut closely,
allowing good leg action. The feathers from the bottom should be cut as
far *front* as the thighs set, which re-
moves all unnecessary adornment, and
gives the cock a chance to fight a
long battle without becoming fatigued
from that source.

ROUP.

___

The Greatest Enemy to Poultry.

___

The Causes of it and Some of the Best REMEDIES.

___

Roup is the most relentless, and in the end the most persistent of all poultry plagues. It is an inflammation of the air passages, which often pushes its presence into the cleft palate, the mouth and eyes.

In its incipiency, or at first it is only a cold or catarrh, but as it advances toward the last stages it gets ulcerative, and is termed ulcerative catarrh, or diptheritive roup; and is claimed by Drs. Spaulding, Johnson and others, to be closely allied in all its essential characteristics to malignant diphtheria in the human subject.

The origin or causation is due to filth, insufficient or improper food,

wet or damp roosting places. Either
or all combined is cause sufficient to
produce roup in its first stages.

The first symptoms are a fullness
about the eyes, slight running at the
nostrils and a snuffling kind of sneeze.

When you see these symptoms, go
to clearing away the cause as fast as
possible. In the first stages the bird
will get well without treatment if
the cause is removed. If wet or damp
chilly weather is the cause we can
only partially relieve it by giving
them good dry houses kept thoroughly cleaned and disinfected, and given
a little tonic in their food. But if
the food is musty or foul with some
poisonous bacteria in it make a change
of feed, for if you do not stop it here
the next stage will set in.

In the second stage the eyes and
nostrils get closed by a tenacious glue
like exudation. The bird breathes
deep and difficult, the mucous collects
in the wind pipe, and all over the
openings into the air passage yellow
ulcers, cheesy exudations are deposited, causing the bird to cough, and
often ends in suffocation.

I have had considerable experience
with roup in this stage, and will give

the remedies that I have found to cure every time. Coop all your sick birds in good dry warm coops; keep the coops well disinfected by using carbolic acid, one part; water, ten parts; or carbolic acid, two parts, coal-oil, six parts; or one part sulphuric acid and sixteen parts water. If either is used the coops will always be clear of that odor which always accompanies roup. There is no disease more dreadful, none so unpleasant to treat as roup.

Take each bird and clean out nostrils and throat, and wash off all mucous that may be under the wings or on the face, comb or feathers about neck and head.

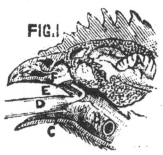

FIG.1

Take a syringe like D in Fig. 1, (This syringe can be obtained at the D. G. Bird office for 25 cts.) and syringe the nostrils as shown in Figs. 1 and 2 with one of the following solutions:

Solution No. 1.—One gill crude petroleum, one gill kerosene and 25

drops of carbolic acid; about 2 drops
of this in each nostril will do.

Solution No. 2.—Put enough chloride of sodium(or common salt) in one
pint of water to nearly float an egg,
then hold the bird by the feet, head
and comb down, choke it until the
mouth is open then insert in the solution so that the medicated water may
enter the cleft in the palate and go
out each nostril and down the throat.
You can then put some in each nostril as in Fig. 2, so as to be certain
that every part was touched by the
solution.

Solution No. 3.—Sulphate of zinc
¼ oz., chlorate of
potash ¼ oz.. to 2
gal'ons of water,
used as Solution
No. 2 will give sat-
isfaction.   U s e
either of these sol-
utions two or three
times a day, but remember to keep all
mucous washed off as before stated,
and keep the bird out of all draught
of cold or damp air.

Kerosene alone injected in the nos-

trils is good.   Camphorated sweet oil
is about the best remedy for roup in
first part of second stage that I have
found when injected in nostrils with
syringe, as in Figs. 1 and 2.

Take turpentine 5 parts, castor-oil
7 parts, and give ten drops to an adult
bird, and inject one drop in each nostril.   Use this three times daily.

Give one dose each day of the following: For an adult bird take ten
drops brandy, four drops tincture of
iron and one grain of quinine.   Small
chicks one-fourth this for a dose.

When the bird seems to be very
weak and you want a quick stimulant
give 8 drops brandy, one drop laud-
nam and a little red pepper, dilute
with a little water to avoid strangling
the bird.   To small chicks give less.

If the bird is costive give one roup
pill night and morning, and feed of
the following: Hot wheat bran cakes,
mashed potatoes and fresh meat of
some kind, livers are good.   The last
feed at night should be cracked corn.

Each one of these remedies are

(5)

good and you can use the most handy
to get.   Only use one at a time.

ANOTHER REMEDY.

U e a solution of chlorinated soda, or carbolic
acid, diluted. Use syringe. The proper syringe for
this purpose can be procured at any drug store, used
for toothache. The tube is curved at the small end.
Inject into the nostrils and bathe head and eyes
with hot salt wa er. Give a pinch of copperas.

ANOTHER REMEDY.

Catch the fowl and give it one tablespoonful of
castor oil, add two drops of paregoric to prevent
cramps. In a little whi'e after giving the physic,
give a pill composed of two grains of quinine and one
grain of piperine. Give these every two hours until
the fever is broken. If that doesn't break the fever,
then give two grains of antipyrine in a pill every
three hours. Alternate. One time give the quinine
and piperine, in three hours give the two grain pill
of antipyrine; give this until the fever has declined.
Use solution for wash as in above remedy and keep
fowls in the dry.

ANOTHER REMEDY.

As soon as discerned the fowl should be placed
by itself in a clean, dry box with plenty of straw.
The head, neck and throat should be washed, and
the eyes should be thoroughly rinsed with warm water in which a little salt has been dissolved. Give a
half teaspoonful of dry black pepper. Supply with
soft food—a little bread soaked in ale is beneficial.
When he begins to improve place him in the sun for
a short time each day. If he continues to rattle, give
a teaspoonf. l of cod-liver oil and keep his box clean
and supply with fresh straw each day.

ANOTHER REMEDY.

For roe, and all putrid affections take finely pul-

verized fresh burned charcoal and new yeast each
three parts, pulverized sulphur two parts, flour one
part, and water sufficient to mix well; make into
boluses the size of a hazlenut and give one three
times a day. Bathe the head, eyes and nostrils with
warm milk and water.

ANOTHER REMEDY.

Compoun 1 Licorice Powder, 3 oz; Powdered Cubeb
2 oz; Powdered Anise seed, 1 oz; Culorate Potash, 2
oz; Hydrastis powdered, 1 oz. Mix and use teaspoonful in feed for thirty hens. This is a first-class tonic
for fowl exposed to Roup.

CHICKEN POX.

Symptons: Su all putrid ulcers covering the head
and neck. The mouth and throat also become badly
cankered. The eyes swel shut and in this condition
the f wl remains until death brings relief. This
disease is very contageous.

Remedy: Make a solution of chloride of lime; remove the scabs and annoint, avoid getting in the
eyes. Sweet oil, camphor and turpentine will cure
and not endanger the sight.

ANOTHER TREATMENT.

Make a strong so ltion of warm water and salt and
with a soft, fine sponge wash the head and neck,
thoroughly rinse the eyes; carefully scrape the mouth
with a small sharp stick to remove the canker and
with the fore-finger rub salt well pulverized into the
mouth and throat. Mix equal par's of sweet oil and
tu pentine a id apply with a feather to the head and
neck.

PIP or GAPES

Is a common disease among youn r f wl, particu-
larly tr ublesome during warm weather, caused
ma n y by filthy rans. This dis-ea; will be detec ed
by the towl holding up its head and gasping for
breath.

Remedy: Take a feather and strip it to within an inch of the feathered end, dip in turpentine, and gently put it down the fowl's windpipe, not his gullet. After turning the feather once or twice draw it out and it will be found to be covered with small red worms. These as well as those that remain will be destroyed by the turpentine. A small piece of camphor gum put into the drinking water will also prove beneficial.

APOPLEXY

Sometimes occurs from over-feeding but most frequently from lice breeding in the ear lobes and affecting the brain. Fowls with this disease will be seen to stagger and fall back or forwa d.

Remedy: Syringe the ear with sweet oil and camphor and bleed the comb.

CHOLERA.

Drooping of the wings, slimy coating of mouth and throat, caused by enlarged liver, suddenly dropping dead from roos'.

Remedy: Give a dose of sweet oil, camphor and turpentine mixed. Smear the roosts and water pans with turpentine and mix a 1 ttle with the food.

RATTLES.

This is a disease caused from over-heating and cooling too suddenly, colds, etc.

Remedy: Swab the throat with a'cohol.

LIMBER NECK.

Symptons: Fowl cannot hold its head up and if not attended to immedi tely has not long to live; caused by fowls eating maggots.

Remedy: Three or four drops of turpentine in a little wat r is recommen el to k 1 them at once.

A GOOD TONIC.

Put one-half pound of sulphate of iron and one ounce of sulp'uric acid into two gallons of water. Put a teaspoonful of this to each quart of drinking water.

Useful Knowledge.

Fowls should have a scalded mash in the morning. Bran is good if scalded with vegetables added; throw in a handful of pepper. Feed it in a crumbly state; feed grain at night.

Laying hens should not be fed too much corn as it is very fattening. It also produces fever and makes them unfit for laying.

Never duck a hen in water to break her from setting. Coop her up with a male and she will quit the third day.

Feed at regular hours and keep the hen house thoroughly cleaned; whitewash two or three times a year.

A very few lice on the young chick's head will kill it. Appy salty meat grease externally.

A hen is at her best at three years old

Never breed fr m a stag or pullet under ten months old.

Dew will kill young chicks. Never

turn them out until the sun has dried up the dew.

Give your fowls a dust bath occassionally. Use a box filled with dust or powered charcoal.

Hens too fat will lay soft shell eggs. Feed more vegetables, crushed oyster shells, and lime to furnish grit for forming shell.

Give your fowl plenty of grassy range. If this cannot be had, spade up the ground so they can have plenty of fresh dirt to scratch.

Move about your flock carefully, as excitement is very unfavorable to egg production.

Chain your dog in the poultry yard at night. Prowlers will catch his scent and keep away.

Hens' teeth will be found in the gizzard,—sand, gravel and like substances are the teeth—don't fail to keep them sharp.

Raw chopped onions fed at night are said to be a preventive of R up. At any rate it is a wholesome food.

Lettuce is a quick growing and choice green food.

Chop green clover fine and feed to all fowls confined in yards.

Don't compel fowls to eat snow in winter to quench their thirst. Keep plenty of fresh water.

The wide awake game breeder is among his fowl early in the morning and late in the evening.

Drinking water in the winter should neither be hot nor ice cold, simply cool and fresh.

The best scare-crow on the poultry farm is a good gun in the hands of a good marksman.

Look well to your young chicks in wet weather.

Keep your young chicks pretty well in the shade until they are five or six days old.

Dry earth is a splendid disinfectant and deodorizer. Keep the floor of your hen house covered with it.

Carbolic acid dropped on a hot

shovel and held in the hen house is a splendid disinfectant and disliked very much by lice.

A FEW DON'TS.

Don't give a cock physic when he has food in his craw.

Don't overwork cocks at any time.

Don't give them solid food during the first three or four days of confinement.

Don't let them out of doors in cold weather if the ground is damp.

Don't over feed.

Don't allow them to remain in dark quarters.

Don't use musty straw.

Don't use a poor quality of food.

Don't forget to weigh them every morning.

Don't handle cocks roughly.

Don't try to get sick cocks in condition to fight.

Don't give away more than 2 ounces to make a match.

Don't allow your friends to handle your fowl.

Don't sit cocks in the sun for at least four hours before the time of battle, as it causes them to "loosen up" and become soft.

Don't think you can whip a main of cocks with a main of stags at even weight.

Don't think you can teach a cock to fight.

Finally, don't think you are the "whole show" for smart people can usually be found in the "small tents." Don't under rate or over rate anyone. Get your birds in the best condition; handle them properly, and bet your money when you think you are right, and if you can't stand losing money get out of the business, because you can not win all the time. Potter's field is full of gamblers who couldn't stand the gaff. Be as game as your gamest cock, and don't bar a cocker if he has a string of victories to his credit as long as the Queen of Eng-

land's pedigree.   Every man and every cock has a stopping place. Allow
the inextinguishable lamp of reason
to guide you in all matters, and do
not permit prejudice to interfere with
judgment.

*   *   *

PART III.

Pit Dogs.

Pit Dogs.

How to Train and Handle Dogs For the Pit With Rules Governing Matches.

Also Diseases, Symptons and Remedies of the Canine Family.

Every trainer has his own system of preparing a dog for the pit. "Old Rhody," the ᴀoted English dog trainer, says when you are matching your dog to fight you must be careful and study the condition of the dog, whether you sign articles to fight in four, six or eight weeks.

Should he be fat or flabby you must allow him six or eight weeks. The best method of bringing a dog in condition is to commence by giving him a strong purgative, but care should be taken to determine whether he is well cleaned out. A strong and useful medicine for this purpose is calcined magnesia. It should be carefully placed in his food and the quantity must be all owing to circunstances. Some trainers give a tablespoonful each day for a week; others give the same quantity for two days; others repeat the dose in two days.

Calves feet and sheepsheads are considered very nourishing food for a dog while being trained. Place them in an equal quantity of water and boil them as long as possible, or until you can shake the bones out of them. Then procure a quantity of wheat bran and scald it, then mix the bran and the soup together and feed to the dog, cold. Feed on that for two or three weeks, according to the time you have got to put him in condition; he should not be fed on hard food more than two weeks. The last two weeks you must get good rump beefsteak and broil it very rare, then take bread and slice it and toast it dry, mix the dry toast with the steak, cut very fine. Do not give him over a

tea-cup full of water each day, and if
you find he is feverish and wants
water, get one quart of Irish moss and
boil it in two quarts of water, strain
it, and give about a tablespoonful of
the liquid when you feed, night and
morning. When you commence to
work your dog, give him about half
an hour's work at a time and increase
his work as you go along. You can
judge how much to feed and how
much work he ought to do. Do not
work him too much, one hour's hard
work is enough for any dog. If he
works good for one hour he will fight
three hours. If he does not lose flesh
fast enough for you, do not feed him
so much. A dog should not be taken
down too fast, one pound a day to
start with and less as you come near
fighting. You must weigh your dog
before and after work, so as to know
exactly how he gets along.

When you have given him his work
rub him well from the point of his
nose to the end of his tail, also legs
and breast – rubbing with the hands
surpasses the brush, towel, or any-

thing of the kind; in case the dog needs washing, do so with alcohol, and be sure to rub him dry with the hands.

A fighting dog shoul i be physiced prior to commencing training on Terper's mineral; and after, castor oil for one week. He then sho ld be walked two miles and return, the distance should be increased every day until he covers ten miles.

After each day's walk the dog should be thoroughly rubbed dry with a turkish towel and then hand rubbed.

A dog should not be fed until after he has been walked or exercised in the morning. The food must consist of chopped beef a id no water but a little tea or ale according to the proportion and weight of the dog. The tea allays the animal's thirst and cools the blood thereby preventing him from becoming feverish, while the ale strengthens him.

In the afternoon of each day the dog must be either put on a tread-wheel, which is better than the wheel which revolves since the latter keeps the dog lop-sided and only works one set of muscles, whereas the treadmill gives full action to the fore feet and keeps his body in full play. The treadmill must be carpeted in order to prevent the dog's feet from blistering.

A dog should be kept on the treadmill not longer than sixty or seventy-five minutes.

The dog must be always blanketed in and out of doors and the blankets must be changed on his return from a walk.

After he is taken from the treadmill he must go through a severe hand rubbing.

After a dog is trained and he has been through the weighing process before the battle, he should be fed on sponge cake dipped in sherry wine and then have thirty minutes rest before pitting him.

Before he is put in the pit a dog should be washed in luke-warm water with washing soda, which takes off and relieves him of any poison or pernicious drugs, if any have been rubbed on him.

After being washed the represeata-
tive of one dog takes charge of his
opponent's dog until the referee orders the men to make ready.

† † †

Police Cazette Ru'es.

1. To be a fair scratch in turn
fight.

2. Both dogs to be tasted before
and after fighting, if required.

3. Both dogs to be shown fair to
the scratch. Both dogs to be shown
head and shoulders between each
second's legs.

4. Both seconds to deliver their
dogs fair from between their legs,
from beginning of fight to the ending
and not to leave their corners until
the dogs are fighting.

5. A time-keeper to be chosen in
the pit; half minute time to be allowed between every fair go away;
twenty-five seconds for sponging;
and at the expiration of that time the
time-keeper shall call, "make ready;"
and as soon as the half minute te ex-

pired, the dogs to be delivered, and the dog refusing or stopping on the way to be the loser.

6. Should either second pick his dog up by mistake, he shall put it down immediately, by order of the referee, or the money to be forfeited.

7. Should anything pernicious be found on either dog, before or after fighting in the pit, the backers of the dog so found to forfeit, and the person or persons holding the battle money to give it up immediately when called upon to do so.

8. Either dog exceeding the stipulated weight on the day of weighing to forfeit the money deposited, and the dogs to be weighed at the place of fighting.

9. Should any police interference or any disturbance in any way, the referee shall name the next place and day by day until the fight be at an end.

10. Both dogs to be washed in their own corners in warm water with soap, soda, and if required, rinsed off with luke-warm water,

11.   The toss for washing; whichever may lose shall bring in the dog and wash him, and after being pronounced clean and dried, then the other dog shall be brought in at the expiration of five minutes and washed in the same water, each handler to produce two clean towels, which shall be exchanged by each party.

12.   If both parties cannot agree on place of fighting then the stakeholder shall name the place.

13.   Should the authorities interfere, or prevent or stop a battle, the referee, if he be appointed, or else the stake-holder shall have full power to name the next time and place of fighting.

14.   On the referee ordering the dog's men to make ready, the handers must hold their opponent's dog and let them loose. After the attendents handle their own dogs, but under no circumstances shall the attendents handle and let go their own dogs until the signal "let go" is pronounced.

15.   In all cases of interference by

the authorities, if the dogs are to fight at stipulated weights the referee shall have full power to insist on the dogs being again weighed and the said weighing shall take place if possible within thirty minutes before the time named by the referee.

16. Should there be any after interference the referee shall insist on the dogs again being weighed day after day, and neither shall be allowed to exceed the weight their owners agreed to fight at.

17. The bets to follow the stakes in all matches and the referee's decision to be final.

Treating Sick Dogs.

If a dog while training should be subject to fits, or what is known as the staggers, at once throw water on them, if convenient. If not, bleed in the neck if you have lancets. If not, with your knife slit the ears, which you can cause to adhere together again; or run your knife across two or three bars next the teeth.

Dogs sometimes contract fever by
want of exercise and too high feeding. Calomel, six or eight grains; or
in an obstinate case, turpeth mineral
or yellow-mercury six to eight grains
in a bolus, or drop it on the dog's
tongue.

Scotch snuff steeped in gin is infal-
lible for the removal of fle s, but
must be used with great care, and not
above a teaspoonful of snuff to a p'nt
of gin, as the cure, if overdone, is
deadly poison.

If a dog is affected with lice use a
small quantity of mercurial ointment,
reduced bv adding hog's lard to it,
say an equal quantity, rubbed along
the top of the dog's back never fails.
The greatest care should be taken to
keep the animal warm.

Dogs contract various diseases, and
few persons know how to administer
cures and remedies. The following
are some of the ailments dogs are apt
to suffer, together with their symptoms:

Stupidity; restlessness; the tongue
becomes of a dark color, and much

swollen; the animal is also constantly
rubbing its jaws with its paws.

INFLAMMATION OF THE BOWELS.

Symptoms: Dullness of appearance
and eyes; loss of appetite; lying on
the belly, with outstretched legs,
pulse much quickened; scratching up
of the bed into a heap and pressing
the belly on it; desire to swallow
stones, coal, etc.

Treatment: Bleed most freely, till
the dog faints away. Clap a blister
on the pit of the stomach. Give aloes
fifteen grains and opium half a grain.
Repeat dose three times a day. Bleed
after twelve hours, if pulse rises
again and continue dosing and bleeding till either the dog or inflammation
gives in.

CANKER IN THE EAR.

Symptoms: Shaking the head and
holding it on one side, and vio'ent
scratching of the ear.

Treatment: The ears should be
well washed with warm water and
soap and then syringed out with a

solution of sugar of lead, in the proportion of about a teaspoonful of the
lead to a pint of distilled or rain water. The washing should be repeated
twice or thrice daily and the bowels
of the dog kept open by a daily laxa-
tive; if these remedies fail, a seton
must be run through the back of the
neck and strong doses of aloes given
every second day.

WORMS.

Symptoms: Fetid breath, voracity
or total loss of appetite, violent purg-
irg, or obstinate constipation, with
great emaciation, sometimes fits. One
of the ordinary symptoms is the dog
dragging his fundament along the
ground.

Treatment: Give first day a small
pill formed of Venice turpentine and
flour, from the size of a very minute
pea to that of a small marble, according to the size and age of the pup.
The former will suffice for Blenheim
or King Charles pups, Italian Grey
hounds, &c.; the latter for Blood-
hounds, Newfoundlands, Mastiffs, &c.

The second day give a small dose of
castor oil; a teaspoonful to the smal-
ler, a tablespoonful to the larger
breeds; in neither case, however,
quite full. Third day, give nothing.
Fourth day, turpentine as before.
Fifth day, the oil. Sixth day, nothing; and so on.

Aloes are useful for dislodging
worms from the rectum, as they pass
down the intestines almost un-
changed; but powdered glass is the
safest and most efficacious; give it in
pills formed with butter and ginger,
and covered with soft paper.

DISTEMPER.

Symptoms: Loss of appetite, dullness, fever, weakness of the eyes, a
discharge from the nose, a short hus-
ky cough, discharge from both eyes
and nose, a peculiar and fetid smell,
emaciation, sometimes fits.

Treatment: Bleeding is the most
useful and that pretty copious; give
an emetic and follow it up with a
gentle purgative; if—as is generally
the case when the above treatment

does not effect a cure—inflammation
of the lungs supervenes, you must
take more blood, give more aperient
medicine, with occasional emetics. If
the animal become weak and is ap-
parently sinking, give mild tonics, as
gentian, quinine; and if he will not
eat, put some strong beef jelly down
his throat. A seton in the back of
the neck is often useful, but should
not be used indiscriminately.

DIARRHŒA.

Treatment: Wait a day or two to
ascertain if the discharge will cure
itself; if it continue, give castor oil
with a few drops of laudanum.

COSTIVENESS.

Treatment: Change the diet; give
gruel and slops; and let the dog have
full liberty; boiled liver will be found
useful. If these measures fail, give
small doses of castor oil.

Conditioning a Dog for the Pit.

By request of Bro. Alex W. Cummings under date of Jan. 13th, 1903, to contribute an article on my way of conditioning a dog for the pit, I hasten to give you what I consider the best that years of experience have proven.

First, see that your dog has a bright eye, and cold nose, then give him a good dose of worm vermifuge that you know will kill all worms in him, follow with a dose of salts two hours later, thus getting his system clean. The time of training your dog deperds entirely upon the condition he is in when you take him up, three weeks is the usual time devoted to training.

First week, give him a ten mile run each day, or one hour's work on a treadmill, not too fast, feeding him a pint of soup for breakfast, and raw, lean meat for supper after all work is over.

The second week, give your dog his ten miles daily, or an hour on the treadmill, and same feed, but give

him twenty minutes of this each day;
put a big cat in a sack, tie it to swing
four f.et from floor, put a muzzle on
your dog and let him work on it, give
him the same work up to within thir-
ty-six hours of the fight, when give
him absolute rest.

See that his eyes are bright and
nose cold, keep your eye out for the
dope and if he is bred right you have
an even chance of winning your
battle.   H. R. P. MILLER,
              Croton, Ohio.

Fourteen Day's Exercise for Cocks.

(By TOM HOWARD.)

After taking a cock up make an
examination of his condition of flesh
to determine the amount of physic;
20 grains of cream of tartar to a cock
carrying heavy flesh. Trim feathers
from the vent and apply cottonseed
oil sassafras oil. in equal parts, over
vent and under wings to destroy any
lice that may be on the bird. After
physic has performed the require-
ment clean your coop and bed lightly

with straw. The following morning feed a teacup of mush and milk or bread and milk. In the evening begin your work out. Start him in with 15 flirts and drill him across the table 15 times. Increase the work to 75 times each, as the cock will stand it. Feed one morning with tablespoonful of hulless barley and one-half white of boiled egg; second morning barley with a little apple chopped fine; third morning, barley and onions chopped up fine. Feed of evenings, yanky corn and best grade of wheat alternately. Give three beaks of water after each feed.

For cleansing the beak, gills and comb, feet and legs, use alcohol two parts and extract of witch hazel one part. Every third day turn a hungry hen in feed room on straw to scratch, to keep cocks on edge and cause them to work feed off.

In following the above feed and exercise, judgment must be used, as all cocks do no. work or feed alike.

Mountain
Eagle

Pit

𝒳

Games

Have proved themselves to be the
gamest, the most complete, the
most beautiful, the best bone,
the surest cutters, and the surest
winners of any strain of Game
Fowls in America. Have plenty
of fine -   -   -

Cocks, Stags,
Hens - and - Pullets

Ready to ship at all times. Eggs in
season. Correspondence solicited.
I have plenty of stamps. -   -

Address,

W S. CHURCH,

Summit, ⋈ ⋈ N. C.

Proprietor of
GAME † POULTRY † YARDS
And Originator of
The Famous Mountain Eagles

R. W. SMITH,

Brandon, Vermont.

Breeder
Of ¶ ¶

Smith's
Crackerjacks,
and
Tanner's
Hummingbirds

The above strains are second to none
and I guarantee them to win or
die trying. . . . .

Stock For Sale at all Times.

Eggs $3.00   per   13,

C. M. Mahone,

Hazlehurst, Ga.

Breeds and
Sells - -

PIT GAME FOWL

GRIST GRADIES, GRIST CHAMPIONS,
CRESTED WHITES, SHAWLNECKS,
HENNIES, BROWN AND SPANGLES
WARHORSES, GEE DOMS AND
BLUE WHISTLERS. . . .

Old and Young Stock for Sale

EGGS at $2.00 per 13.

Satisfaction Guaranteed
Or Money Refunded

Hook's Games,

Reds
Doms
a n d   G r a y s .

But few strains of fowl have as good
a record. They have been used
in nearly all the import mains in
this section for the last six years
and never at any 'ime lost a majority of their fights. Such a
thing does not come by chance;
it takes kicking.   .   .   .

- PRICES REASONABLE -

EGGS $2.50 per Setting.

W. F. HOOK,
Hardinsburg,   -   Ky.

Wm. L. Allen,

Breeder of
Allen's Celebrated

Round Heads
Knob Comb Reds and Grays
and Grist Champions.

These strains have won a majority of their battles against the leading cockers of Mississippi and have never failed to win a majority wherever fought. Against Moore & Ginn and the Ruckers, of Georgia, Jan. 18-19-20, 1903 they won 19 out of 21 battles in main and hacks at Vicksburg, Miss.

SEND FOR CIRCULAR.

W. L. ALLEN,

MARTIN, - - - - **MISS.**
Claiborne County.

Claude A. Ham,

250 Second Street

Memphis, - Tenn.

Breeder of

Southern
Athletes.

Cocks, Stags, Hens, and Pullets for sale. I'ave your Egg orders booked for early shipment. Get your brood stock direct from headquarters. I rices right.

WRITE AT ONCE.

Wade Johnson,

Spencer, Ohio.

MAKER

OF . .

FINE

Hand Forged

Damascus - Steel - Gaffs.

For clean cutting, strength, lightness
and reliability, these gaffs cannot
be equaled. Made on scientific
lines to do the greatest possible execution. A battle is half won
when you have tied on a pair of
my gaffs. A trial will convince you.

New York Regulation $3.00
New York Regulation with to hooks......3 50
Half Drops 3.50
Full Drops 3 50
Cincinnati Skeleton socket 3 50
Front Drops 4. 0
Jaspers 4 00
Spurs knifs or case .... .75
Spurs for blades 1 0
Set of Muffs 1.00
Dubbing shears......................1.00
Cutting out Shears..................1.00

Retirement Stock Farm,

(IN THE VALLEY OF VIRGINIA)

Offer for sale

Grist Champion and Grist Henry W. Grady

Pit Games.

Have bred them in their purity for the past seventeen years. Nothing gamer or better fighters. All stock guaranteed. Pointers and setters of the highest breeding and from field trial stock. Our Mr. Geo. W. Herring is President of the Va. Field Trial Association.   .   .   .

No Circulars   Write for what you want.

Herring Brothers,
Bridgewater, Va.

S. J. McCracken,

Tecatur, Texas.

Breeder Of PIT GAME COCKS.

Shawlrecks
.Of the winning kind.

Grist Champions
, s fine as silk.

Warhorses
Of the shuffling sort.

McCracken's Rough Riders
Come Reds and Greys, and as fine as
ever shaded the earth.

Everything bred on good farm walks
and all cocks and stags walked
for the pit.   †   †   †   †

Also Breeder of

POLAND CHINA HOGS
Of The Finest Strains.

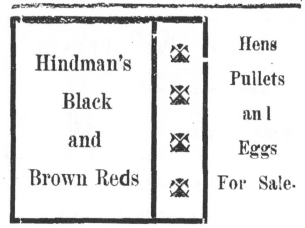

Are a strain of strictly up-to-date fighting fowl. They have fought from three to seven mains every year for the last twenty years, and have their first main to lose. I have never been able to supply the demand for my fowls as many of our best cockers know. My prices are low, considering quality; but I am out to compete with no one. Those wishing to buy common stock for little money are at liberty to do so.

Cocks and Stags for Mains
A SPECIALTY.

S. A. HINDMAN,
Rush Center,   -   Kansas.

Howard's Flashlights
and
Groves Old Family

**BRED IN THEIR
PURITY. . . .**

Two † Celebrated † Strains

That win 75 per cent. of their battles. The most aggressive fighting cocks living, deliberate cutters
and cocks that are never whipped
until dead.   .   .   .   .

PRICES.

Cocks $7.50 to $15.00; Stags $3.50 to $5.00; Hens $4.00
each or three for $10.00; Pullets $2.00 each or three
for $5.00; Eggs $2.50 for 13 or $4.00 for 26.

Stamp for Catalog.

†   †   †

T. A. HOWARD,
3237   N.   Western   Avenue.
Chicago, Ill.

Alfred · Horner,

MANUFACTURER
OF . . . .

Steel Spurs
Of Every Description

EVERY PAIR
WARRANTED

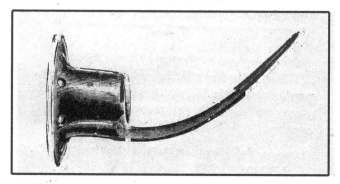

I also grind razors and put them in shape, ready for use. Write for circular and price list. . ; .

Box 168,
South Milwaukee, Wisconsin·

Years Ago

I began breeding Game Chickens and Bull Terrier Dogs. I started with the determination to breed the very best Cocks and Dogs possible. The public was quick to appreciate the high quality of my stock and my business has increased very rapidly, and to-day my cocks are heading the yards of some of the largest breeders in the land, and my Dogs are the best to be had in America to-day. Now you can get Eggs this season from any of the following yards at

$3 00 Per 15 or $5 00 Per 30.

HENRY'S IRISH BLUES, HENRY'S HIGH COMBS, HENRY'S TARTAN TASSELS, HENRY'S GREYS AND HOPKIN-SON WARHORSES.   .   .

Young Stock After Sept. 1st.

Gentlemen, I appreciate your order no matter how small, and you will get a SQUARE DEAL if you will send me your orders.   -   -   -   -

Try my Roup Cure at 25c a package—It will do the Business.

F. G. HENRY,
The Game Chicken Man,
Marietta, Ohio.

A. M. CORY,

Acushnet, - Mass.

BREEDER OF
PURE . .

GRIST CHAMPIONS
BLACK & TANS
AND COMBINATIONS.

Young stock before Oct. 1st, $5.00 per trio. Eggs $2.00 per setting or three settings for $5.00. For prices on other stock write.

EVERYTHING
GUARANTEED.

Ed. Hossfeld

Topeka. Kansas.

BREEDS AND
FIGHTS . .

RACEHORSES,
WARHORSES,
GEE DOMINIQUES
AND I. X. L. WARRIORS.

These strains have a record hard to
equal. I have traveled with
them north and south, pitted
against the best of them, winning the lion's share wherever
fought. . . . .

EGGS $2 per setting;
3 settings $5,

HORNETS

BRED AND WALKED.

On good farm walks away from all
others. Have held their own for
15 years in all company. They
contain the best blood of the south
and are fast fighting, always push-
ing and never taking the defensive
side of battle. Correspondence
solicited. . . . .

The renowned Thurmond Dogs
pure; the ¾ English, ¼ Thurmond.

Guaranteed Game to the Last

ORIGINATED
AND BRED BY

J. A. THURMOND,

Hardys, S. C.

Frymire Smoke Balls, Doms, Grist Gradies, and Mugwumps.

Four Better STRAINS Cannot be Found·

Our cocks never fail to win in our hands and we have fought against the best in the land. Our patrons everywhere are winning with them. We shall be pleased to quote prices on anything in our line.   -   -

DR J. B. FRYMIRE & SON.,
Frymire,   ·   ·   Ky.

John Dale,

Eastondale, ⋈ Mass.

† † BREEDS † †

PYLES, Reds and Blues,
Boston Roundheads,
1-2 Derby 1-2 Imported
Brown Red,
Shenandoahs
and Dominiques.

* *
*

My cocks have whipped everything in this part of the brush and are winning for my customers everywhere.

I ship nothing but first-class stock. Write for prices on cocks and stags that will be guaranteed to win or die trying.